Parenting Teens

Strategies for Helping Children Handle Life Challenges

(Parenting Guide to Parenting and Marriage Sustenance)

Adrian Nguyen

Published by Rob Miles

© **Adrian Nguyen**

All Rights Reserved

Parenting Teens: Strategies for Helping Children Handle Life Challenges (Parenting Guide to Parenting and Marriage Sustenance)

ISBN 9781990084331

All rights reserved. No part of this guide may be reproduced in any form without permission in writing from the publisher except in the case of brief quotations embodied in critical articles or reviews.

Legal & Disclaimer

The information contained in this book is not designed to replace or take the place of any form of medicine or professional medical advice. The information in this book has been provided for educational and entertainment purposes only.

The information contained in this book has been compiled from sources deemed reliable, and it is accurate to the best of the Author's knowledge; however, the Author cannot guarantee its accuracy and validity and cannot be held liable for any errors or omissions. Changes are periodically made to this book. You must consult your doctor or get professional medical advice before using any of the suggested remedies, techniques, or information in this book.

Upon using the information contained in this book, you agree to hold harmless the Author from and against any damages, costs, and expenses, including any legal fees potentially resulting from the application of any of the information provided by this guide. This disclaimer applies to any damages or injury caused by the use and application, whether directly or indirectly, of any advice or information presented, whether for breach of contract, tort, negligence, personal injury, criminal intent, or under any other cause of action.

You agree to accept all risks of using the information presented inside this book. You need to consult a professional medical practitioner in order to ensure you are both able and healthy enough to participate in this program.

Table of Contents

INTRODUCTION 1

CHAPTER 1: IT STARTS FROM YOU: ESTABLISH YOURSELVES! 3

CHAPTER 2: COMMUNICATION WITH A MODERN CHILD. 13

CHAPTER 3: MAINTAINING A CLEAN HOME 31

CHAPTER 4: RAISING A CONFIDENT CHILD 44

CHAPTER 5: BEING READY TO TAKE CARE OF YOUR CHILD 50

CHAPTER 6: HOW YOUR CHILD DEVELOPS IN A NORMAL WAY 55

CHAPTER 7: A REAL FRIENDSHIP BETWEEN YOU AND YOUR CHILDREN 59

CHAPTER 8: THE IMPORTANCE OF DISCIPLINE 67

CHAPTER 9: HOW TO BRING UP A CHILD WITHOUT STRESS AND HARM TO THE CHILD 77

CHAPTER 10: WORKING WITH YOUR FEELINGS 87

CHAPTER 11: HOW PARENTS CAN HELP 94

CHAPTER 12: SLEEP 100

CHAPTER 13: MOTIVATION 103

CHAPTER 14: WHAT YOU NEED TO TEACH YOUR DAUGHTER 109

CHAPTER 15: THE ARRIVAL OF THE CHILDREN 113

CHAPTER 16: CHILD PARENTING METHODS................... 124

CHAPTER 17: HOW TO TALK TO YOUR CHILD ABOUT MOLESTATION... 131

CHAPTER 18: CHILDPROOFING YOUR RV 137

CHAPTER 19: HELPING THE CHILD TO OVERCOME HIS SENSORY PROBLEMS.. 144

CHAPTER 20: A CONFIDENT TEEN IS LESS TROUBLE 150

CHAPTER 21: KIDS NEED SOMEONE TO TALK................. 159

CHAPTER 22: CHALLENGES 3 AND 4 - CHANGES IN YOUR LIFESTYLE AND RELATIONSHIP.. 163

CHAPTER 23: BEING A SINGLE PARENT DOES NOT MEAN RAISING AN UNSTEADY CHILD.. 169

CHAPTER 24: SINGLE DAD WITH TODDLER: CUTTING TOXIC TV TIME.. 176

CHAPTER 25: ON BEING A GOOD DADDY THE FIRST YEAR 183

CONCLUSION 191

Introduction

This book contains proven steps and strategies on how to tame your toddlers especially when their behavior becomes out of hand. As children move from being babies to toddlers, they are amazed at the unbelievable freedom that appears right before their very eyes. Suddenly, they can stand, walk, eat, explore, and run on their own. They have the ability to think on their own, touch, feel, manipulate objects and a whole lot of crazy things a parent could dare imagine.

This book is created with parents of toddlers in mind. There is no more important responsibility in life than that of being a parent. Parenting is a full-time job, regardless if you have an outside, corporate career or not. You may take time off from your job, but you are never off the clock when it comes to being a parent.

In this book, you will learn how to tame, discipline, and deal with challenging toddlers, understand their behavior and what needs to be done when they are becoming uncontrollable, and other techniques to help discipline this interesting little person.

Thanks again for downloading this book, I hope you enjoy it!

Chapter 1: It Starts From You: Establish Yourselves!

It is saddening to some extent to witness the abundance of parents who seemingly are not prepared or eligible enough to become parents. It is even more saddening and distressing to witness the abondances of children who, quite obviously, haven't undergone a proper upbringing, doubtlessly because of the category of parents we have just mentioned. The lack or absence of a proper and healthy upbringing reflects on children in multiple ways. It produces a cocktail of manifestations which, no matter how much they differ, do revolve around a mutual characteristic: unpleasant, unacceptable, unhealthy and negative manifestations.

We believe it's the time to consider this matter with more seriousness and more in depth. It is undeniable that establishing a family is one of the important purposes of marriage, and is being pursued and aspired for by millions of couples and spouses worldwide. Nevertheless, truth being said, not all those aspiring to become parents and longing to have a children are necessarily eligible or worthy of handling such a critical responsibility. Yes this statement may sound cruel and too "bitter" and harsh to be absorbed, yet is the inevitable truth, because of which the rate of social conflicts maintains an exponential elevation. These social conflicts represent a broad spectrum, ranging from the simplest wrongdoings such as a child saying a bad word to a friend (though this situation by itself is not simple. It hurts!), to the most serious and dangerous, even dangerous to elder people, such as mugging and theft, bullying, harassment and even murder.

Given that we are interested in introducing this subject with as much frankness as possible, we will attempt to cover all the essential aspects and highlight the common problems before proceeding to the methods of solution and construction, which will be depicted in more details in the following chapters.

Taking a look onto married couples, we can realise they basically divide into two main groups: Those who wish to build a family with children, and those who are satisfied with the small family that comprises the couple itself – and not willing to have children for reasons that vary from a couple to another.

It is very interesting to realise that, among those not wishing to have children, there exist so many who are sophisticated and knowledgeable enough in regard to healthy parenting. They can be logically assessed to be absolutely eligible. However, provided that they know enough about parenting, let alone about its responsibility, they have accordingly made the decision of not bringing any child to life as they do never wish to compromise their duties or to show any sort of dereliction, even if unintentionally, to their children. In other words, these people love their children and care about them so much, that they prefer keeping them in a "better world" to bringing them to this life and not giving them as much as these parents expect themselves to give.

On the other hand, amongst the larger proportion of married people who long for having kids, it is appealing to detect a plenty of those who are ignorant of the simplest basics of parenting and upbringing. They have no mental or cultural preparation. They are even unaware of their own responsibilities, and even when they are, they cannot handle them altogether. Nonetheless they still want to go through the parenting journey and to experience taking care of someone else while they still in need to look after themselves and their own lives first!

Unprepared, irresponsible and inconsistent parents are not expected to demonstrate any good skills in parenting. Quite often, parents happen to be prepared, yet in the completely wrong and unfavourable way.

We shall also declare in this context the abundance of parents who at first keep showing eagerness and passion towards becoming parents. Afterwards, once this is accomplished, they start to share endless complaints, regrets and negative wishes. This attitude is demonstrated usually by mums, especially in the communities wherein the responsibility of children and household are considered to be handled exclusively by the mother, with the father's role being confined (by these communities) to be outdoors bringing money to the house. Like, seriously!

Addressing these people-complainers, we would like to introduce the question: "What did you expect?" Simple as that! You people had better not make the decision of becoming parents until you vividly recognise your roles, responsibilities and what parenting is actually about, and until you become confident and aware enough of yourselves that you would not transform into consistently whiny individuals by the time your child is born or your offspring multiplies.

We shall emphasise that there is no aim to dissuade anyone from parenting, nor to discourage or scorn anybody, rather it is about enlightening you about the importance of obtaining as much knowledge as possible, and the importance of self-preparation at all aspects.

As the title of this chapter suggests – it all starts from you. When we say "you" we are actually addressing both of you as a couple. The first and most essential point to always bear in mind, especially you, future fathers, is that parenting has and is never the responsibility of the mother solely!

To a misfortune, a number of communities around the world impose the responsibility of parenting on women in the first place. These communities instil this concept in people's brains and programs their intellect to believe in, adopt and accept this concept without modifications or arguments. This has led millions of involved women to find themselves having to "sacrifise a lot" for the sake of marriage and becoming good mothers. These sacrifices happen to be as serious as having to quit their jobs or very often, their education and academic life! On the other hand, husbands and fathers are very often found to be pursuing their life goals and ventures quite normally and almost similarly to what they would do if unmarried (exceptions are still present – so many fathers out there have their lives dramatically changed due to their children, sometimes to the worse...). As a matter of fact, parenting, as well as other serious life plans, does entail some sort of sacrifice. This sacrifice is nonetheless to be given by both the father and mother, and it does not have to reach the extent of sacrificing one's life or abdicating any of the other significant life plans and goals that are aspired for by one of the spouses and sometimes by both.

It is definitely the responsibility of both ends. The father's role has never been confined to his outdoor investment of his efforts to bring an income to the family. The children need their dad as much as they need their mum. They would like to talk to him, have fun and spend so much time with him similarly as they do with their mum. It is the father's duty to guide his children, teach them life lessons, construct their personalities and instil in them manners and values. It is his duty to do so in collaboration with his wife towards a fruitful upbringing. He is not at all supposed to have nothing but a financial-material connection between his children (that is he buys them what they want, pays for their living and that's it!). He is not at all supposed to be completely nonchalant and indifferent when he witnesses his children making mistakes and exhibiting some wrongdoings. It is his duty here to meddle and put an end for his children's misbehaviours. It is his responsibility to enlighten them about what should never be done and why, rather than awaiting their mother to take action all by herself and to invest her efforts for the sake of rectifying their children's attitude without the least assistance from his end. It is undeniable that numerous familial cases are continuously reported and spoken about in which children consistently complain about the fact that "they don't feel they have a father". This condition is usually attributed to the misconceptions of paternal roles instilled in brains of the involved fathers, making them assume it is fine to be continuously absent from home and away from children, and it is bringing no harm as long as "we are absent for the welfare of them!"

After realising the importance of both of you in the parenting journey, comes the step of mental and personal preparation in a way that is appropriate enough to keep you away from regretting becoming parents and/or complaining about your kids' problems and the dilemmas relevant to them. Many parents, including potential ones, prefer seeking parenting courses and books to establish themselves properly and efficiently. This is an action to be applauded for indeed. Based upon that, this book has been created with hope of being in convenient service upon necessity. The following six chapters will consider what comes next towards becoming parents who are good enough to bring up satisfied, healthy children and create an overall happy comfortable familial atmosphere. It is interesting to state that, although speaking about parenting responsibilities can seem to imply difficulties, complexities and obstacles to some extent, you would later realise that what parents should learn is actually not that difficult nor too complex to comprehend. It is mainly about full awareness, discipline and appropriate estimation of the demands and factors of good parenting.

Chapter 2: Communication With A Modern Child

Parenting already is a very difficult job for a person, couple that with having to communicate with a teenager or adolescent that doesn't want to communicate with you. Then, you know you have an arduous job on your hands. One aspect of parenting where a lot of parents have failed in is communicating with their kids, and who can blame them; they are just mirroring the way they were spoken to as a child. Parents don't have any problem giving instructions and facts to their kids, trust me! They excel at that. Things like, "Go and clean my car." Or: "Make sure you look out for cars before crossing the road." Of course, parents excel at this form of communication. Do you want to know where parents fail? When it comes to the emotional stuff, parents really suck at communicating their intense feelings – or when their child's feelings are involved? Many parents say they don't just struggle with communicating with their child, they complain that even when they initiate a conversation, their kids only reply with one-word answers or nods, or the monosyllabic yes/no answers. The real struggle is actually having a true conversation with your kids when they feel like they can actually tell you what it is that bothers them, and you as their parents can advise them on what to do and in some cases just listen.

Before I go on to tell you how to foster communication between you and your kids, I would like to let you know why kids, especially teenagers, don't like to talk with their parents. I know you might be thinking, "But my kid is not even a teenager yet." Well, I am glad to tell you it starts from their preadolescence years. So why don't teenagers talk to their parents? You might ask. You see the problem is not that they are broken, have terrible parents or are not even loved. At least in most cases, that is not the problem. Like Kate Russell, an experienced teacher and guide for secondary school students, said in one of her blog posts for Peaceful Parents, Confident Kids :

"In every case, I queried, 'Is there someone you can talk to about this at home?' And almost always the answer was a resounding, 'No!' with rationales like, 'They just wouldn't understand' or 'They would be so disappointed in me!' Which would come flooding out with tears that fell uncontrollably. It often seemed that this realization itself was to them sometimes more painful than the life event they were dealing with."- Kate Russell.

It turns out that after Kate did some research on the reason why this happens, she found out that the problem stemmed from their childhoods. While our kids are growing up, regardless of if what we as the parents do is coming from a place of love, they come to the conclusion that we only show love and approve of them if they were of good behavior and had outstanding achievements. The reason why they tend to think this way is based on how the parents choose to discipline their kids when they make a mistake or do something resoundingly stupid, is that it forces you as a parent to do things like take away their toys or ground them. All of these are fine, but the mistake parents make is that they do not communicate with their kids on why they are being grounded or punished. Rather than say something like, "Oh my God! Did you just break another mug? Go to your room, you are grounded." You can decide to instead say, "What! Did you just break another mug? (Because of course, who wouldn't be that way?) Come here. Clean up this mess." Then, you can sit them down and try to explain to them why what they have done is bad. It is better than just telling them that what they did is bad. You can still decide to ground the child by saying, go to your room and think about what you did. This is a far better approach than the just punishing and not letting them know just why and how it affects everyone else. Of course, the personality of every kid is different, and they might require a different method, but the overall concept is to let them know that there is a consequence to their actions and that it might affect just more than them. Then, in the end, they should always know that you will love them no matter what by always pulling them back in after a rebuking session.

Here are recommended ways to make sure that your kid knows that he/she can talk to you:

Choose discipline over punishment

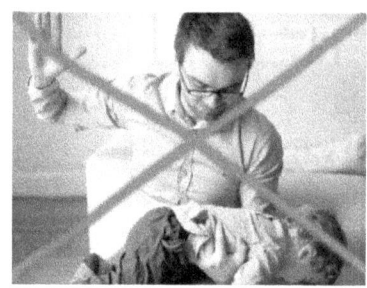

When your child displays a behavioral pattern that is abhorrent and/or unusual, before you impulsively send them to the dungeon, you should at least try to understand why they did what they did and then let them know why the way they are reacting to it is bad. This is probably one of the best chances you would get to nip a bad behavior in the bud, so why waste it? This way, you communicate to your child that they can approach you when things don't seem to be going how they expect, and also when they are excited about something, they will be inclined to let you know, too.

Acknowledge their emotions

Sometimes we know that our kids are just being little brats about their emotions and we can sometimes make the mistake of just dismissing those emotions, by saying things like, "Oh, stop being such a brat" or "You are just saying that because you are still a kid." These are ways in which we push them away gradually. Even if the way they are acting is just a result of childish emotions, we should find a way to acknowledge that we know how they feel and that it gets better with time. That way, when they face the real adversities that come during the teenage years, then they will know that they can always speak with their parents.

You should note, however, that all of these are general ways to deal with fostering good communication with your child. It varies from child to child, as they have different personalities, upbringing, environment and so many more factors. When it comes down to it, though, this is the basic principle behind being in a good communicative relationship with your kid.

Now that you know how to make sure you don't prevent your kids from being able to communicate with you, you might wonder just how to communicate with your kids. Here are a few ways I have learned over the years that work:

Using approaching statements

Generally, these are the statements that allow your children to want to say more. This could work on almost anybody, but focus! We are talking about our children here! The whole idea is to let your child know that you are really interested in what he/she has to say. These kinds of statements allow your children to know that you accept and respect him/her; it makes it feel more natural to talk to you. Some of the kinds of "approaching statements" you can use include:

Oh, I see,

How about that!

Wow! Really?

I really would like to know more,

What! No way.

Amazing.

Woah!

That's cool.

Are you serious, so what happened next?

Now, I am not saying you have to fake this sort of response when you are with your kid, because trust me, they can easily sense when you are not being sincere with them. What you need to do is practice actually listening to them when they speak and when they expect to get a response from you; if you have been listening, you will be able to respond in a way similar to the ones listed above. Also, you should know that in making them feel that you care, eye contact is actually necessary. If you make an exclamation and you are not looking up from the cabbage that you are slicing, it would not matter that you listened. The keyword here is attention .

Tell your kids what to "do" a lot more than "what not to do"

A  lot of parents actually make the mistake of always telling their kids what not to do, while this is necessary and okay sometimes. One thing we as parents forget is the fact that if we keep telling them what not to do, how then do they know what to do? Bear in mind the fact that it is not every time that doing the opposite of what you are told not to do becomes the right thing to do. Plus, if as a child you hear a lot of what you should not do, you tend to do those things most of the time. Also, it would help the self-esteem of your kid, if you refrain from always telling them what not to do. Instead, you should tell them what you expect them to do more often. Imagine how you would tell, say, your friend or a relative what not to do. You probably would instead suggest what they should do. You would say things like:

"Hey, come on. Why not put your clothes on the dresser, they will stay less wrinkled that way?"

"Drive carefully, Bob!"

So, when talking to your kids, your statements should sound more like,

"Hey, go clean your room."

"Pick your clothes off the floor or hang them on the dresser instead."

"Come on, John. Play your games after you are done with your assignments."

There are some things that are reserved primarily as a warning and you should tell them straight away not to do, like:

"Don't play with fire. It would burn you."

I know two parents who, during the rare tantrums of their son, say the exact opposite of what they want him to do. Sometimes, their son watches cartoons on a tablet. In the case when he needs to take a break, and he begins to act up and throws a tantrum, they tell him all the harm from the excessive viewing of the cartoon and then add: "Okay, look further at your cartoon, but know this is your choice and your health, and you are deliberately ruining it, so let's continue..." Maybe this is a slightly manipulative method of communicating with your child, but I assure you that it works for them. The child stopped crying and watching the cartoon. And he is sure that it was his own decision.

Let your kids know when you are serious with your request

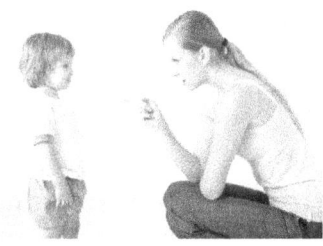

Sometimes, parents wonder why it seems like their kids ignore them when they give instructions or make a request for them to do something. The truth is, as human beings, regardless of whether or not he/she is a child, we all like to feel like we are in charge, and as kids, one thing children like to do is explore their limits. Children are just figuring out the extent of their environment and that includes just how much authority their parents have over them. Therefore, this is why sometimes when they are fully engrossed in whatever it is that they are doing, it is not uncommon for them to ignore you and be one with what they are doing.

Moments like this are very important to us as parents, because it is moments like these that help us cement our status as parents. When you want your child to do something, you have to make it clear that it is important that they do that thing; you should not make it vague. The best way to do that is to first make sure that you have the attention of the kid, and then speak with a firmness that shows you mean what you are saying at that moment.

Therefore, a good request would sound something like this, "Hey, Michael. I need you to go clean the sitting room, please. You know your dad will soon be back and he doesn't like it when the sitting room is dirty." This will definitely be received better than you yelling, "This is the last time I will tell you to clean the sitting room." Remember we are trying to foster better communication between you and your kids, not alienate them.

Also, from time to time, you should learn to appreciate your child when they go out of their way to get something done. It lets them know that you actually are aware of their actions, and it will help them trust you even more.

Kind words are essential

This should be a no-brainer, but most parents still get it wrong. You should refrain from using abusive words towards your kids, apart from the potential to make your child a bully by teaching him ways in which he can make another child feel bad about him/herself. You also risk pushing your child away and hurting his self-esteem. You should avoid calling your child names, like "stupid boy" or saying things like, "you are acting dumb, put it in the jar."

Statements like this will make your child feel disliked, and in the end, he/she will cease to communicate their feelings with you.

Instead, you should learn to use kind words with your kids. This would breed better self-esteem for your child, and also, you will be able to communicate effectively with your kid. The way you should speak with your child should sound more like this:

"I warned you that was going to happen. But it's okay, get the dustpan so we can clean this up. At least, now you know what not to do."

If you speak to your child like this, it would definitely make them more open to talking about some things with you.

Like I also said above, you should learn to use kind and appreciative words on your kids.

When they do things right, you should learn to say, "Thank you," "I love you,"

"That is some nice 3D model." Doing things like this will definitely make you a better person in general and definitely a better parent than you already are.

Acceptance is key

In the end, you want to let your child know that he/she is accepted by you. This way, they can be their true self around you and not just who they think you want them to be. This certainly makes your child see you as someone whom they have to impress all the time just because you are their parent. It makes them see you as someone that they can show all of themselves to without the risk or fear of being judged. Your child will feel safe around you, and that is something we all want for all our kids.

When you get in the habit of always judging your kid or lecturing them about this and that, after a while they begin to resent being around you—they dread every moment they spend around you and all they want is for it to end. This could let them seek the attention they need elsewhere, which is very bad for you and for them.

Say, for instance, your child needs to take a medicine but he/she doesn't seem to enjoy taking it. Rather than try to force it on them, say things like, "Don't worry, I will be here while you take it. You need to take it so you can get well. You can take it slow or at once, as long as you can take it." You should always try to encourage your kid.

Now, when I say to accept your kid, I definitely do not mean you should accept all of their bad behaviors. Instead, what I mean is that when you discover that they have a certain behavior that is bad, you should try to communicate it to them in a way that doesn't make them feel inferior or hated. You should always find a way to understand what your kid is going through at all times, even if you are sure that he/she should do what you are saying.

Chapter 3: Maintaining A Clean Home

Cleanliness is close to godliness. Or at least that is what my Grandmother, my mother, and, despite my best efforts, even I now say. No one wants to walk into a house or room to find that their child is living in a pig's sty. Clothes strewn everywhere, dishes and old food left out all over the kitchen, and dirt and mold everywhere. It just isn't healthy to live in an environment like that.

Of course most of us did at one stage or another live like that, but that is no reason to say that our kids should ever know. The saying 'do as I say, not as I do' can be used to great effect here when trying to impart to your child the importance of cleanliness in their life. So let's get straight into what and how we should be teaching our teens before they leave home.

Lesson #3: Basics of Cleaning

If your child is lucky enough to have coasted through life never having to clean up after them self it is time for a wakeup call. When moving out of the house your child needs to know some basics about cleaning so that they can be self-sufficient if living alone, or teach them the cleanliness habits they will need to fit in when living with others.

I personally lived with one or two people who were completely clueless when it came to cleaning when I moved out of home. They were alienated. Neither lasted very long in the house and people really held it against them that they were messy. We had to constantly baby them to keep the house from turning into a garbage dump. It is unfair to expect that other house mates will clean up after you like a parent would, and many people will not stand for it.

What we want teach our teen here is that cleanliness is not just for themselves, but that it will be appreciated by those that they live with. Whether that is housemates, boyfriends, or girlfriends. Being a clean person can be a huge positive when looking for somewhere to live and so we as parents will do well to build clean habits into our kids.

Suggested Steps to teach basic cleaning habits

1. Cleaning their bedroom

Key lessons that need to be imparted here are:

When to change sheets and pillow cases

How often to vacuum

Why folding clothes and making the bed is important (because anyone that sees their room will be judging them on it)

The importance of letting in natural light to avoid damp and mold

It is easy enough to let your child maintain a messy bedroom when they are living at home as closing the door means that you never have to see or deal with it. However it is very important to instill in your child the importance of cleanliness for general health. Not washing sheets, and living in a damp and moldy room can cause skin conditions, breathing problems, and all kinds of other sickness.

If that is not a lesson enough in itself, I personally found that the biggest helping hint for my son was telling him that girls would not want to spend any time in his room if it looked like a tornado had hit it. I got a few of my girlfriends when they were over to enforce the same idea to him and, wouldn't you know it, he now keeps his room relatively tidy at all times.

2. Cleaning the kitchen

So that your child does not make themselves or anyone that they are living with sick, they need to know how to maintain a clean kitchen. The lessons that you need to teach here are:

Cleaning products required - Jiff, Mr. Muscle, Oven Cleaner

Washing the dishes - Hot water and detergent to kill germs

Making sure that your child maintains a relatively clean kitchen is a vital lesson that all parents need to teach. Food preparation is an area that many mistakes can be made that result in sickness for your child and others living with them. By knowing these basic skills you can be confident that not only will your child be less likely to get sick when cooking themselves, but that they can help others that they are living with to avoid making similar mistakes.

3. Teach the use of basic appliances

Your child needs how to use the following 3 items at a minimum before leaving home:

Washing machine

Vacuum

Iron

Dishwasher

This does not mean that your child has seen you using them. It means that you need to get them up from their computer or seat in front of the TV and walk them through how these things work. What washing powder to use, how to empty the lint catcher, how to change a vacuum bag, where to read on a vacuum which bags they take, the settings that your iron has and which clothes that applies to, and how to iron their clothes are all necessary lessons.

You can either set a schedule to go through one item per day or simply call your child in every time you are using an appliance that you want to teach them about. This is often met with resistance initially, but after a few viewing sessions you can entrust tasks like turning on the dishwasher, changing the vacuum bag, and ironing to your teen without worry. . Cleaning the bathroom

When leaving home your child should be knowledgeable of how to clean a bathroom in the following ways:

toilet bowl should be scrubbed with a toilet brush and detergent regularly

Shower cleaned with Jiff, Mr. Muscle, or other shower cleaners at least every 2 weeks

Floors swept or mopped to remove bacteria every week to 2 weeks

Bathroom and toilet mirrors should be cleaned using a glass cleaner, and wiped with a paper or cloth towel

Toothbrush and toiletries to be replaced every 2 - 3 months

Because of the moisture accumulated from the showering or baths the bathroom is susceptible to mold and bacteria. Teaching your child how to properly maintain a bathroom ensures that they will recognize when their bathroom needs to be cleaned and that they have the skills to do so.

Key Takeaways

Cleanliness says a lot about a person, and I know personally that I would be disappointed if either of my children's messy habits were seen as a failure on my part as a parent. So instead of leaving anything to chance make sure you take the time to show them in detail how to use necessary appliances, and teach them why it is unhealthy and potentially dangerous to live in a messy room and cook in a dirty kitchen. This is all basic knowledge to us as parents but it needs to be drilled into our kids before they take that first step to independence.

Lesson #4: The use of basic appliances

Some of our teens have a knack for avoiding learning about how certain appliances in the house work. It is a great plan when they have parents such as us who will clean up after them and let them get away with their ignorance. But ignorance of how things work once they leave the safety of home is not acceptable.

For this reason we need to make sure that our teens are equipped with knowledge of some basic appliances that we use to clean.

Vital appliances I recommend teaching your teen about:

Your child needs how to use the following items before leaving home:

Washing machine

Vacuum

Iron

Dishwasher

This does not mean that your child has seen you using them. It means that you need to get them up from their computer or seat in front of the TV and walk them through how these things work. What washing powder to use, how to empty the lint catcher, how to change a vacuum bag, where to read on a vacuum which bags they take, the settings that your iron has and which clothes that applies to, and how to iron their clothes are all necessary lessons.

You can either set a schedule to go through one item per day or simply call your child in every time you are using an appliance that you want to teach them about.

Key Takeaways

This is often met with resistance initially, but after a few viewing sessions you can entrust tasks like turning on the dishwasher, changing the vacuum bag, and ironing to your teen without worry. Operating these appliances is vital to living a normal life once you're teen leaves home. So although they may fight you on whether it is necessary for them to learn these things while at home, you need to be tough and drill these lessons into them while you have the chance.

Lesson #5: Basic Home Maintenance

While living on their own, your teen will need to know how to fix small home appliances such as a clogged vacuum cleaner, a clogged toilet, or a damaged electrical appliance. This could save them from having to call a professional to deal with the problem, which could save them a lot of time and money. It will also potentially save you from getting calls at all hours of the day asking for advice of how to fix things over the phone.

Suggested Steps to Achievement

Some basic things that I have learned are necessary to teach your children are:

How to change a light bulb

Where a circuit breaker is in the house, and how to turn back on after a surge has turned power off

How to unclog a vacuum cleaner

How to unclog a toilet or sink with a plunger

How to de-ice a freezer

How to reset a modem to troubleshoot basic internet problems (literally unplug for 1 minute and plug back into the wall)

Once again, some of these things we as parents will take for granted but your kids may not otherwise know what to do so it is up to you to teach them before they leave home.

Key Takeaways

The greatest benefit of learning how to deal with the maintenance of home appliances is that they potentially save money that would have otherwise been used to hire the services of a professional. Being self-reliant in this way builds confidence in children helping them to make the transition to adulthood. In some children learning such skills can spark an interest that will lead them to more and more advanced fixes that could see your children becoming more knowledgeable than you. It is always a great feeling when you cannot fix something and knowing that your teenager is capable and competent enough to do it for you.

By teaching your children basic skills such as these you can have confidence that they will be able to manage on their own. It will also let you rest easier knowing you will not receive calls in the middle of the night asking for advice on very minor easy to deal with problems.

Chapter 4: Raising A Confident Child

Confidence is the foundation of a child's maturity. It is also the key to his success in the future. What you feel about yourself influences the way you act. When you feel good, it is easier for you to get along with others and feel comfortable with them.

Here are some tips to help your child develop self-confidence.

The first thing that you need to do is to allow your child to realize his uniqueness. If you look in the mirror and you like what you see, you feel comfortable with who you are. You think of great things about yourself, including being worthy of love and having the ability to make things happen. Parents serve as a mirror of their child's personality. As a parent, you need to let your child see the good in him. As he grows up, you have to remind him of his worth and his abilities.

Maintain parental attachment with your child. A child must feel loved and valuable from infancy. He needs to be constantly caressed and touched. You may not be able to constantly respond to your baby's demands, but it's important that you are there for him most of the time. If you develop a constant connection with your child from infancy, he will grow up with a special connection with you and that will remain intact in his mind no matter what happens along his journey to adulthood.

You need to improve your own self-esteem. If you have problems in your past that can affect your parenting, you need to face them and move on. You don't want to let your child suffer the consequences of your past mistakes and failures. It will interfere with your effectiveness as a parent to your child. And if your child sees that you don't possess the confidence needed to succeed in life then you will hardly help him develop his own self-esteem.

Reflect a positive image to your child. In number 1, you learned that you serve as a mirror of your child. You need to do it in a positive way but that doesn't mean that you have to tolerate his misbehaviors. You have to learn to allow your child to realize his bad habits and help him overcome them so as to become a better person someday. This way, your child will be comfortable enough with you that he would be willing to rely on you to tell him when he's not behaving well.

Spend some quality time with your child by playing together. By playing together, you are making your child feel that he is worth of your time. It will also make him realize that he is valuable to you. The more you play with him the better he feels about himself.

Make your child feel special. Playing with him may seem to be a random activity but your child is more sensitive than you can imagine. He will sense if you are genuinely interested in being with him or if you are just trying to make it appear that way. So focus on your child whenever you spend time with him. This is the best time to get to know your child in a deeper way.

Encourage your child to hone his talents. Once you get to know your child's interests, you will find out the things that he does well. Let him enjoy the things that he loves doing and motivate him to improve his skills. If you recognize your child's abilities, he will feel it and he will become more comfortable with himself.

The child's self-concept and values will be nurtured by the significant people in his life — family, teachers, coaches, and friends. As a parent, it is your responsibility to determine who among these people can make or break your child. Allow your child to be exposed to others but monitor every individual that he spends more time with.

Choosing the best school for your child is a very important task you would not want to ignore. You have to carefully consider the academic curriculum of the school as well as its overall environment. Some schools may help him boost his personal abilities while some can only make him feel frustrated in competing with other students.

One of the best ways to hone your child's confidence is by giving him a sense of responsibility. Assign him some household duties. By doing so, you are making him realize that he is an important part of the family. As he gets started, you need to work with him. Allow him to get familiar with the task until you can leave him to do the task by himself.

Self-confidence is not inherited but acquired. Don't misunderstand its meaning by making it look like it's a requirement to his growth. You don't measure it like temperature that you can simply say that his confidence rises or falls at any given day.

Confidence is developed overtime. Just like the way you keep a flower garden, your job as a parent is to nurture what's already in your child; you don't look for something that isn't there. You don't make him someone he is not. Be sensitive to your child's needs and accept his abilities even though they are different from the abilities of other children who are of the same age. Allow his confidence to develop naturally.

Chapter 5: Being Ready To Take Care Of Your Child

Taking care of a child is an exciting part of a person's life. Becoming a parent not only is an honor, but also is a rewarding vocation that many people are given the chance to do. However, with this great responsibility come things that can make you feel stressed. In order for you to become the best parent to your child, you have to be prepared not only physically or in respect to the things that you will need, but also emotionally. Here are some things that you can do in order to reduce the stress of becoming a parent:

Get as much help from your family as you can. Especially if you are a single parent raising a child, you will need as much help both mentally and emotionally as you can. If you have a partner to help you, or if you have the presence of a concerned parent or one of your parents-in-law, then you can ask them for their help once the baby is born. You can also try hiring a nurse if it is possible for you to do so.

You will also need a very strong support system. Basically, what you will be needing is someone who will be there for you for whatever it is you are going through. You will need someone who will be able to help you with all the little problems that you will encounter when you take care of your child. This person might be your spouse, your boyfriend, or even your parents. A support system is vital because if you do not have one, you will most likely feel exhausted immediately, even if your baby is just resting or feeding. With all those being said, you should also establish your own rules regarding times when people would be allowed to visit, as well as rules when visiting. You can actually be susceptible to even more stress when you are visited by too many of your friends and family members, especially in unexpected visits.

Especially on the first month of your child's life, there are a lot of unexpected things that could happen. Therefore, it is important that you clear your schedule. Ensure that you do not have too many plans and that you can give enough time for your child. You can take stress off from you by also telling your friends in advance that you are going to be busy with taking care of your child. Never force yourself to go out and socialize when you know that your child still needs you, or at least if it is something that you really want to do.

You should also not forget yourself. Of course, even though it is important for you to be always there for whatever it is that your baby needs, you should not forget that you also have needs for yourself. Make sure that you get enough time to regularly bathe, maintain a well-balanced diet, and get sufficient hours of sleep every night. You and someone else such as your partner or a person in your support system can work out a schedule wherein both of you will have enough time to take good care of yourselves. Although you will not have the time to start a new hobby, you should allot enough time for exercise, for hanging out with friends, and for a simple "me time" whenever you can get the chance to do so. It is also important that you do not think that you are being selfish when you think for yourself once in a while. You can think of it as when you take more care of yourself, you are giving yourself a chance to be a better caretaker for your child.

Even though at times you may feel that a day with your child is a thousand hours long, you will soon realize that your baby will grow up even before you know it. Therefore, it is also important for you to be prepared for the emotional ride that you are going to go through, from the high joys of seeing your baby take her first walk, getting the fear that you are not doing things all right, panicking that you are now losing your independence, and feeling isolated from your friends with no children. These emotions are very natural and they will fade once you begin your new life with your child.

Chapter 6: How Your Child Develops In A Normal Way

Every parent is concerned about the development of their child, and wants assurance that their child is growing and developing at a healthy rate.

If you are a parent, who has a basic understanding of normal child development you will have a clear understanding of how your child is most likely to develop. You'll have a basic calendar of events to look forward to, and you'll be better able to stimulate your child and encourage and assist them in good and age appropriate growth and development.

An understanding of normal child development can also draw attention to any potential growth and development challenges your child may encounter along the way. As, your child, reaches the chronological age that a particular milestone typically occurs in, then you can foster that growth by providing opportunities for your child to learn.

For example, at 12 weeks, an infant who is following the typical path of normal child development is learning to raise their head and shoulders to 90 degrees when they are lying on their belly. A great way to encourage your baby to develop the physical strength to reach this milestone is to allow them ample 'tummy time.'

When your baby is alert and content, lay them on a blanket on the floor; then get right down on the floor with them. Call to your baby, hold a toy out for them to look at, find a way to entertain them for short periods of time so that they have a chance to build up those neck and shoulder muscles.

But don't push it. When, your baby starts to get fussy, pick them up. Try and fit in few time throughout the day to allow your baby to explore the world while on their tummy.

Normal child development is gauged, in a child's cognitive development as well as their physical development. At around 6 months of age, babies are beginning to develop object permanence, which means that when an object is taken out of their sight they still remember that it exists.

A great way to help your baby develop this cognitive milestone in normal child development is to play peek-a-boo. Cover your face with a blanket and then whip it off with a smile. Your baby will be thrilled to see you re-appear again and again.

Eventually, as your baby begins to figure it out, she will take the blanket off your face, because she will suddenly be in on the joke. She will have developed object permanence.

Babies also love to practice object permanence by dropping toys and watching you pick them up. So the next time your baby throws his toy off the high chair for the twentieth time, remind yourself that you are helping him develop his cognitive abilities by continuing to pick that toy up and put it back on the high chair.

A child masters an impressive list of accomplishments during infancy and toddler-hood. They begin life unable to lift their chin or effectively communicate their wants and needs. But week by week babies follow a chain of events developing skills and achieving milestones as they make their way along the path of normal child development.

Being aware of these milestones allows us to be more aware and more involved in the growth and development of our child.

Chapter 7: A Real Friendship Between You And Your Children

Remember how many bad friendships you have had in your life? How many people have let you down in your life? How many have betrayed you? How many times have you sought the advice and comfort of a best friend? Did your best friend actually make you a better person? Did he/she remain with you through thick and thin, or did they end up being forgotten in the tides of time? What does good friendship mean to you?

Well, you can answer that one all by yourself. For me, good friendships are something that allow me a sense of freedom and allow me to have have fun. I don't need to hide my true self and good friends understand me, without passing judgment on me. They will feel embarrassed by my idiot pranks just as I will by theirs. They will be the proudest cheerers during my victories and they will be the last to leave my home during times when I need them. They will know me, correct me, and know when something is wrong, showing concern - but without imposing their views on me. They have no hidden agendas. Your kids can be your best friends, with a few differences.

First, they are not your age. Remember that they don't have the same life experiences as you have. They don't understand the world as you do. Many parents fall into this trap of treating their kids as adults, which will rob them of their childhood. Once you treat your kids as adults, they will try to behave and act like adults before being ready for this process. Though it is funny to see them acting all grown up, while still under 3 to 4 feet tall, the problem is that they will not have been through all of their development stages.

They will be kids just for a little while. Ask any parents and they will tell you how fast children grow and how they will miss them being little kids. So, why rush? Your kids don't need to accept responsibilities when they are not ready. They don't need to listen to conversations they are unable to fully comprehend. They need to be around toys. They need to spend time with other kids their own age, while you may be more interested in toys for big boys, or girls. You should treat your child in accordance with their age and try to remember that little people are just that – kids that have not yet learned to think like grownups.

When I am around my friends, we usually take decisions together. With your kids, it is not always a democratic process, where they need to have a say on everything that you decide. Sometimes, it is good to let them decide and have their own opinions, while on many other occasions, it is not practical to let them be part of the decision-making process. They will not process the same information as you do, because they are not adults. So, it is clearly useless to try to explain yourself and try to make them understand why you had to do something for their own best interests. They don't see things in the same way that you do. This doesn't mean that you should be always use the excuse "Because I say so!" You should be open enough to talk to them about those things that are proper for their age.

Give your kids full freedom within their development stages and be appropriate for their age. Allow them to take decisions, answer their infinite "why" questions, be there when they make mistakes and come running back home with tears in their eyes. But, don't cut corners. Don't rush them into growing up and treat them as your own friends. Give them responsibilities as they grow – different age appropriate household chores - allow them to take care of different things and be part of your household activities like paying the bills, making sure that all the insurances are up to date and other things like that but show them in kid terms that they understand.

Set the family hierarchy clearly, and show them that you are in command and that they are to follow you rather than the other way around. However, do it with respect and caution. Try to win your arguments with your experience and example, and don't try to overpower your kids with threats or by being too defensive. Kids are smart. They will respond immediately to your own style of leadership. You can be their best friend, but still remain a leader.

Respect their identity, who they are and how they develop this identity. I made this mistake myself. I tried to push my own life expectations onto my son when I was his age. I remember thinking to myself: "He will never make the same mistakes I did." "He will be a much better soccer player than I was" but he is a great tennis player. And, he has to learn from making his own mistakes. I can help him to understand why things happen the way they do and try to teach him how to avoid these problems, but kids will be kids and they will make mistakes. These are what they learn from, rather than having parents who don't let them be themselves.

Respect and value each of your children's identities. Be surprised by them and their talents and celebrate them whenever you can. Though you have to be the strong foundation of their lives, you also need to watch as they discover their own identities. Let them feel good about who they are instead of feeling downtrodden by your rules.

It is important to develop this relationship of trust and friendship before they become adolescents. At that stage, they will seek their own independence and try to stay away from you as much as they can. Remember the age when you felt ashamed of your parents, even though you still loved them? This is a reminder that you are not always going to be considered as their "friend" and that their interaction with their peers should also be part of their learning process, providing you know that they are safe.

Though this is a phase that tries your patience, they will grow out of it and come back to you. The stronger your educational bases are set at an early age, the easier they will find the transition from being a small child to being a responsible adult and they do need space in order to achieve that level headed adulthood we have always wanted them to achieve.

As a true parent, as a true friend, you will let them know that you will always be there for them, no matter what. You will trust what you have built on through their younger years. And at this crucial point in their lives, they will be thankful from a distance. They will be confident in themselves and will let you know about it, by coming back to you when their friends are not there for them, or life has new challenges for which they don't know the answers. Try to avoid using the "I told you so" approach as this will alienate teens who are looking for support, rather than chastisement. They need you to be a constant, their roots, their strength.

Keep listening to them, talk with them, correct and look them straight in the eyes. Allow them to grow, establish a relationship of trust and freedom, and when they become adults, they will be your best friends in return. You have to remember that teens don't understand what it's like to be anything other than the center of their own universe. It's what is natural to them, but when they grow up and love someone more than they love themselves, they understand and know that all you ever did was provide positive support and love for them.

Chapter 8: The Importance Of Discipline

Disciplining your child is just as important as everything else you're teaching them, and sometimes, it's just necessary. This is the part of parenting most parents dread. They see discipline as a negative action because, when they were growing up, discipline was negative for them.

However, you can choose how you discipline your toddler, and it doesn't have to be in line with what your parents may have done, or it can be! That's the beauty of having a child; you get to choose how you raise them.

Before we take a look at the proper methods of discipline for a toddler and the improper ones, let's look at some of the benefits of discipline. Let's shine a new light on this word that's perceived to be negative by many people.

Helps Children Manage Anxiety

As much as they might look like they want to be, your toddler doesn't really want to be in control. They test the limits to make sure their parents are going to keep them safe! When an adult offers positive and negative consequences for an action, it will help the child learn and grow.

Toddlers who have permissive parents will feel anxiety because they're managing their decisions all the time. They never have any direction. Children know they're not able to make the best choices all the time and they want to learn from you what decisions they should make. The lack of guidance and help tends to create feelings of anxiety rather than comfort.

Teaches Good Decision-Making

The right discipline will teach your toddler how to make better decisions. As an example, when a child loses the privilege to ride their bike because they rode into the road, they will learn to make safer decisions the next time they're riding their bike.

Healthy discipline will provide your toddler with the chance to think about their actions and recognize an alternative solution to the problem. Toddlers need to learn problem-solving skills, so they can understand the possible consequences of their behavior and actions.

It's imperative to distinguish the difference between punishments and consequences. When children are disciplined with the right consequences, they will learn from their mistakes. Punishments will tend to teach your toddler you're mean, or they learn how to 'not get caught' when they do something wrong.

Discipline Teaches Them to Manage Emotions

Discipline will help your child learn how to manage their feelings in a positive manner. For example, when your toddler receives a timeout for hitting their playmate, they learn a valuable skill to help them manage their frustration in the future. The goal is for your child to learn to take a time out on their own when they feel really upset.

Other strategies, such as praise, teach your children how to handle their emotions. For example, "You're working really hard to build that tower despite it being really hard to do. Keep up your good work." This helps motivate them to tolerate frustrations and keep going without giving up and accepting failure.

Ignoring is a good way to teach your child how to manage their frustrations, too. When you ignore a temper tantrum, your child will learn this isn't a good way to get what they desire. Ignoring other behaviors, like whining, will show that these attention-seeking actions aren't working and they'll need to find another way to meet their needs when they feel upset.

Discipline Keeps Them Safe

The main goal of disciplining your child should always be to keep them safe. This includes major issues, such as looking both directions before they cross the street, or not riding their bicycle in the street. There should be consequences for your child when they're not taking the right safety precautions.

Discipline ought to address other health issues, such as preventing becoming obese. If you allow your child to eat whatever they want whenever they want, this will create some serious health conditions because children are not able to make healthy choices for themselves without your guidance.

When you use an authoritative approach and tell your child the underlying reason for why they shouldn't do something, it helps them learn to examine the safety issues of an action before they do it. For example, rather than saying, "Get down from there," when your child is jumping on their bed, it might be helpful to let them know it's a safety risk and they could get hurt. This teaches them to look for a potential safety issue in other situations.

Core Components of Healthy Discipline

When most parents think about discipline, they think about punishment. But effective discipline is more than just losing a privilege or having a time-out. In fact, these consequences are not likely to be effective if they're the bulk of your discipline focuses because they're negative. Healthy discipline needs to contain five core components.

#1 Healthy Relationship with Your Toddler

If you don't have a healthy relationship with your toddler, then discipline isn't going to work.

Toddlers are more motivated to listen to what their parents are saying when they respect their parent's decision. The need for having a healthy relationship with your child stems beyond just you. Teachers, step-parents, and daycare providers are much more effective when they have healthy relationships with your child, too.

#2 Discipline's a Teaching Tool

If discipline is just reserved for correcting bad behavior, it's not going to be very effective. If you find you're always saying, "Don't do that," and, "It's time-out time," without teaching them the right behavior, then they won't learn. That means your toddler is more likely to repeat that mistake in the future.

To really help your toddler change their behavior, discipline should be a teaching tool. That means helping your toddler identify what to do. Rather than telling your toddler not to hit their brother, make sure you invest time in teaching your toddler to resolve the conflict peacefully.

#3 Be Consistent

If you only put your toddler into time-out one out of every ten times they hit their sibling, then your toddler's not going to stop hitting their sibling. After all, it's worth the risk of performing the behavior if there's only a ten percent chance they're going to get into trouble.

If you want discipline to be effective, then you have to be consistent.

If you put your child in time-out for hitting every time they hit, then your child will link their behavior with the consequence. Over time, your child will realize that this behavior leads to a consequence they don't like.

#4 Be Immediate

Being prompt about a consequence will help your toddler connect the dots between behavior and consequences. If a toddler doesn't lose their park privileges for a day for hitting someone at the park, then the consequence is not as effective.

There might be times when you can't have an immediate consequence for something. Sometimes, you might not realize your toddler has broken the rules until hours or days later. In these instances, a late consequence is the only option. However, it's important to avoid saying things such as, "Wait until your mother/father gets home," because a consequence that's given hours later is going to be less effective.

#5 Be Fair

If your toddler forgets to put their toys away before bed, and you keep them from playing with those toys for an entire week, your toddler won't perceive this to be a fair consequence. Therefore, your toddler might try to sneak in play when you're not around. Your toddler won't abide by the consequence if they don't think it's fair.

When kids are convinced they're being served injustice, then they will fight you every step of the way. That doesn't mean you need to negotiate with your toddler and give in when they protest about the consequence, but it does mean you should make sure your punishments are not overly harsh.

So remember, discipline is important because it teaches your child to be safe, how to manage their emotions, and keeps them feeling secure. Now, let's look at some of the common discipline mistakes parent make with their toddlers.

Chapter 9: How To Bring Up A Child Without Stress And Harm To The Child

What can you do for your child, so that your toddler can feel confident and protected and can be able to develop his potential one day?

The most important thing parents can do for their children is to give them the impression that the entire world is open to them.

Let's think together: The parent, first of all, gives support, safety, and a foundation from which the child's potential can grow.

The parent puts faith in the child strengthening the child's inner core.

The parent gives love, understanding, and respect. He or she also helps the child to find and discover his own resources and potential.

There is always a balance between democracy and boundaries. In the theory of psychology, there are many opinions of how to "rightly" punish, i.e. how to show the consequences of inadequate actions to the child.

I am one of many psychologists who are AGAINST CORPORAL PUNISHMENT.

For a child whose body is invaded, the world becomes unsafe. Forever. Children who are afraid that they will be beaten will become manageable. And they will lose touch with their authenticity, their strength, and their potential.

Seven Important Points for the Education of a Toddler

1. Freedom is not permissiveness.

2. Any child will seek to push the boundaries.

A cub develops within his limits. And unfortunately, general advice received from others rarely works. What works in the upbringing of your friends' and relatives' children might be useless for your child. Also it is important that any punishment corresponds to the awareness and age of the child.

It is important for us to sense (and to learn from books and articles on child psychology), what the needs of a child are and what tasks should be completed at a particular age.

At 1.5 - 2 years of age a child does not have control over his emotions, feelings, and impulses. The child acts impulsively and imitates others. It is important to tell the child – "DON'T" or "STOP."

Take the child out of the tension zone and refocus his attention on something else.

At 2.5 - 4 years, your child develops a self-consciousness. Your child begins to learn to take responsibility for his actions and their consequences. You need to give the child a moment to think (sitting on a bench, for example). And then help him cope with the consequences (say "sorry," collect the broken glass from a fallen cup, and so on).

At 3.5 - 5 years - respect for the person is very important. To beat, belittle or scold the child, especially in the presence of others, is not recommended. We can say – "Now let's correct what's done," "We'll figure it out at home," or "Let's think together how to behave in the future."

After 5 years, children know when they are breaking the rules. IT IS IMPORTANT THAT THESE RULES BE WRITTEN IN THE HOME CONSTITUTION or that they are given verbally. And it is also important that a decision is made together with the child as to what penalties (punishments) are imposed for breaking the rules. Remember that it is better to punish the child by depriving him of something good rather than by inflicting negative things on a child of any age.

3. Even the most adapted, most obedient child will occasionally make trouble. YOU ARE NOT A BETTER OR WORST PARENTS BECAUSE OF THIS.

4. Do you know what children are most afraid of?

Mom's and Dad's angry eyes! When you are angry, it shows in your eyes. Do not be angry!

5. "Correct" punishment should help the child develop, but not break his spirit.

6. Often kids make us angry because they repeat the same thing over and over again. It seems this is their favorite game. Please remember that some areas of the brain need to develop for the assimilation of experiences. And children do not possess those areas until four years of age, or sometimes even later.

Until then, a child does not learn the consequences of his or her actions. Therefore, any rule requires a minimum of 30-40 repetitions until it becomes ingrained.

7. Children in the pre-speech period (when human speech has yet to be learned) reach out with the help of the physical body. Have you observed how one child comes over to the other on the playground and lovingly hits him on the head with a shovel?

For a child, this is an attempt to establish contact in the only way possible for them. But just remember the child will try different patterns of behavior by watching our reactions.

We should remember that if a child does something physical, stopping it with words is useless. These are completely different languages of communication. Our reaction must be rapid, adequate, and logical.

You may have noticed such situations – a mother slaps a kid, saying "Don't fight!" Or a kid hits his grandmother in the face with all his strength – and she kisses his fist in response. So, the child hits dad, confident that the reaction will be more kissing ... and Daddy, for some strange reason, is not pleased at all. Can you imagine what a strange dual experience the child gets?

So, if the action is performed physically, our response should also be physical. To beat the child in the response to his action is certainly not the answer. Instead, catching the hand of the baby, we squeeze it slightly (gently, painlessly, but firmly enough), look QUIETLY into his or her eyes, and say "I (people, children and so on) cannot be hit." ... And, of course, remember, point 6 (see above).

We need to remember that explaining the rules is one way to establish the boundaries for the child. Until the time when the child says "I" in reference to himself, he can't correlate punishment with himself. Punishment and threat is intimidation, and it is difficult for a child to live in suspense, expecting something terrible.

When punishing children, we should try not to recall all previous misdeeds and mistakes and talk to them only about what we are punishing them for right now. Don't mention everything your toddler has ever done in the past.

The child's punishment must be consistent. For example, don't punish something one day and not punish it the next day.

 When punishing children, insults should be avoided as well.

 To punish a child in the presence of other children or adults is unacceptable.

Regarding physical punishment of a child, there are three rules that express the limitations of what physical punishment can achieve in helping a child develop a proper attitude toward the parent. There are three things you "cannot" do:

1. You cannot intimidate a child with physical punishment.

2. You cannot physically punish the child and take out your anger on them.

3. You cannot physically punish a child older than three years, so as not to degrade their personality.

The punishment for a small child is not so much in words or actions as in the emotions and intonations that color them. Physical punishment does not add anything positive after a sense of fear has already been awakened.

We quarrel, but we are rarely taught how to end quarrels and conflicts. And we carry a load of emotions—disappointment, anger and powerlessness—not letting ourselves let them go. But we should remember that a child does not have the same perception of time, and for them every moment is an eternity.

Our sadness, irritation, and anger are painful for them. Please help your kid and yourself - stay in contact. That way you will make a huge contribution to their future adult relationships.

Think of "rituals" that your family can use in the home to bring about reconciliation. This will help "close the door" to the past and "open the door" to the future. It can be very simple — a secret handshake or a tight hug.

Chapter 10: Working With Your Feelings

When a family is dysfunctional, the needs of the child are not met. Not getting our needs met is incredibly painful, and that pain is expounded when the adults in our lives are unable or unwilling to listen to, support, or nurture us. When we repeatedly find ourselves in this situation, we start to develop coping mechanisms that allow us to defend against our feelings. Shutting out our feelings allows us to survive as children, but we grow into adults that are strangers to our own likes and dislikes, hopes and dreams, fears and desires (Whitfield, 1987). When you have a wounded Inner Child, you must learn again how to feel your feelings. Below is a three-step process to help you to reconnect with your emotions and learn to both feel and share them in a healthy, authentic way.

Identifying your Feelings: Sometimes, the wounds to the Inner Child are so severe that we shut ourselves off from our emotions altogether. We are afraid to feel anything at all because expressing authentic feelings requires a certain level of vulnerability. If you are at this level of awareness with your feelings, then you need to start small. Simply focus on naming and owning your emotions. Get a feelings chart off of the Internet (a simple Google search of "feelings chart" yields hundreds of results, so choose the one you like the most). At the end of every day, take a look at your chart. Record in your journal which feelings you felt that day, and when. If you felt happy, what made you feel that way? If you felt sad, why? How did you handle those feelings? Slowly but surely, you will become more and more comfortable with your own feelings. You'll be able to recognize your emotions without the aid of your chart, and you'll have a new language of emotion to help you share your feelings authentically with other people in your life.

Sharing Your Feelings: Sharing your feelings is a fundamental part of achieving intimacy with other people. When our Inner Child is wounded, however, we learn to be very careful about how we express our feelings. People who grow up in dysfunctional families are often punished for being vulnerable or authentic, and so find it difficult to trust other people with their true feelings. This dynamic separates us from our true selves, and causes us to be manipulative or emotionally distant, sometimes without even realizing it. If you are at this level of awareness with your feelings, then the tool you need to heal is Trust. Slowly but surely, practice opening up to people that you consider close to you. Maybe that person is a family member, a friend, a partner, even a co-worker. Go slow, and go easy. People who have trouble expressing their feelings often "share" their feelings as ideas or opinions rather than expressing them for what they are – emotions. To circumvent this, challenge yourself to use one "I feel" statement every day. Again, make sure to say it to someone you trust, not just anyone. Slowly but surely, it won't be a challenge anymore. Each time your honesty, authenticity, and intimacy is rewarded rather than punished, accepted rather than judged, another wall around your Inner Child is torn down.

Exposing your Feelings: At this third level of feelings awareness, you are able to recognize and honestly express your feelings, but you may find yourself retreating or shutting down when someone else responds in kind. You may find yourself only sharing what you know will be accepted and hiding what you think will be rejected. This level of awareness is only semi-functional. It certainly won't serve you to share everything that pops into your head at every moment (this, too, is dysfunctional in its own way), but if you find yourself keeping secrets from people you are close with, this, too, can be a sign of a wounded Inner Child. It's one thing to draw healthy boundaries around your personal and public life. It's something altogether different to purposely mislead someone because you are afraid that telling the truth and being authentic will lead to negative consequences. Every human person makes mistakes, but in order to have healthy, loving relationships, we must own up to those mistakes. A true friend will never reject you for being honest. A loving partner will never belittle you for admitting to something you are ashamed of. If you are at this level, you must learn to expose yourself to potential conflict.

We often justify manipulative behavior by pretending that we are protecting the other person - "I don't want her to get hurt," you might say, or "I just don't think it's worth the argument," convincing yourself or others that you are being the bigger person and taking the high road by staying silent. This is not authentic behavior, and it's not being honest with yourself. Children can be startlingly direct, and won't hesitate to share their feelings honestly, with no fear of the social consequences. It's to this childlike acceptance of the validity of your own feelings that you must return to. Did you keep a "Secret Diary" as a child? It's time to make one again. Commit to 15 minutes every night before you go to bed, or even 10 if this feels like more than you can spare. In your Secret Diary, on one side, write down anything that you wanted to say to someone that day, but didn't. Write down what you told that person instead of the truth, and why. Then, on the other side, write down what you could have said to that person that would have expressed the truth.

As an example, we'll use the classic "Does this dress make me look fat?" question. In this situation, you are withholding a thought rather than a feeling, but the basic idea is the same. In your Secret Diary, write down that your partner asked you this question, write what you wanted to say, and write what you actually said. Maybe you wanted to say, "Yes, you look huge!" but you said, "No darling, you look gorgeous." And maybe your partner felt so happy and supported, but would it not have been more supportive to be honest and help your partner find a dress that really looks good on them? On the other side of the page, think about what you could have said. "You look huge!" may not be appropriate, but what about "Honestly, it doesn't flatter you at all. Maybe try a different color?" Or "Yes, but what's wrong with that? I think it looks great!" Or "I don't want to hurt you, but yes, that dress is not doing you any favors." There are ways to be true to ourselves without hurting others. After a while, you won't need your Secret Diary anymore – you'll have trained yourself to speak authentically and honestly right there in the moment, and you'll be amazed at how much the quality of your relationships improves.

Chapter 11: How Parents Can Help

Raising a kid with high self-esteem is serious business. It takes time, effort and a lot of wisdom to pull off successfully. But while it is no walk in the park, raising a daughter in her middle years is definitely easier than when she is on her teens. This is why it's important to take advantage of this stage if you want to a rear a child that's ready to take on the world when the infamous teen years come into the picture.

If you have a darling child who obeys your every request without complaints, lucky you! But if you have one who's a bit bossy and demanding, that's completely normal too. The key is to know what to do when they'd need a parent to guide them through the murky waters of growing up.

With low self-esteem among young girls becoming a serious issue today, you need all the tools you can get your hands on to ensure that your child will grow up healthy and confident. Below is a collection of some child-rearing wisdom that can help you help your daughter grow up right.

Love Makes a Lot of Difference

To be the best parent to your child is a tall order but it's not at all impossible. For most kids, all they really need is to know that they are loved unconditionally. Love, after all, is like fuel to your child's self-esteem. When they know they are loved, their self worth is affirmed giving them just the right amount of bravado and confidence while growing up.

Love is Spelled T-I-M-E

For most kids in their middle years, love is often equated to quality time together.

While they enjoy having new friends, they'd still want to be with you most of the time. Make the most of it by giving her your full attention. Be interested with what she's been up to. In fact, you set weekly dates where it's just you and her doing things you both enjoy.

You can watch movies together, go shopping and bake. When she still wants it, you should also make it a point to read to her before bedtime.

Communication is Key

Like with any relationship, effective communication is one of the keys to raising a confident kid. At age 8 or 9 when she may start to encounter tween issues, you have to be there for her as both parent and friend. Always make her feel that she can talk to you about anything and everything under the sun. This means no nagging, no quick judgments and stop feeding her negativity.

Kids at this stage still love to talk and open up. Your job is to listen well and provide advice at the right time.

Support Her Interests

Another way to show her your love is to support her interests. If she wants to join a glee club or a sports team, let her. When you let her do what she does best and pursue her interests, she'll feel more independent and capable. And when she loves what she's doing and she's good at it, high self-esteem will eventually follow. Making everything even better is you supporting her all the way.

When she has an event at a school like a performance or anything that showcases her talent and interest, be sure to be there to show your support. Yes, even if you're busy or stuck with work. You have to make a way if you want a confident, happy and well loved child.

Allow Room for Mistakes

Just like you make mistakes, she will too and a lot of them she will commit in her tween years. Give her enough room to make them. Don't be the perfectionist parent who gets riled up when her daughter fell short of one's expectations. You can be better than that by turning those failures and mistakes into valuable and meaningful learning experiences.

When your daughter does commit mistakes, be sure to choose your words carefully. Never use negative words to reprimand or lecture her. As the proverbial saying goes, "hate the sin but not the sinner." Talk about what she did and not because you think she was stupid or not good enough.

Recognize Achievements

One of the best ways to build self-esteem in a young child is to recognize her achievements no matter how small or insignificant. This will make her proud of herself and what she can do. Those little achievements are also great encouragements for her to keep on achieving more.

While at it, give her praise every chance you get. This will reaffirm her self-worth and boost her confidence even more. You should also recognize her individuality and avoid comparing her to other children altogether.

Kids in their tween years, particularly age 6 to 9, are in the middle of developing their sense of self. As a fertile stage for valuable lessons and new experiences, your job as parents is to help nurture their self-esteem by giving them love and support despite shortcomings, mistakes and failures. At this point, it's all about you using your words and action to teach them about how they should value themselves no matter what people say, the media dictates and the environment impresses.

Chapter 12: Sleep

Sleep is an important element in all people especially children. They must in a sense recharge their batteries effectively with adequate sleep. One of the strongest forms of torture is sleep deprivation. When you do not set parameters for your child to receive enough rest you are in essence putting your child through torture. This torture effects their mental, physical, and emotional growth. When kids do not get enough sleep, you are sending a living zombie to school. This not only makes it hard for your child to learn, but also for the teachers to effectively teach them.

Some Side Effects of Lack of Sleep

☐ Impaired Brain Activity

☐ Excessive Yawning

☐ Cognitive Dysfunction

☐ Moodiness

- Depression
- Weakened Immune system
- Weight Gain
- Cold and Flu
- Type 2 Diabetes
- Accident Prone
- Heart Disease
- High Blood Pressure
- Memory Problems
- Stunts growth

As you see from this exhaustive list sleep plays a key role in keeping your child healthy.

Sleep Suggestions

Create a sleep routine for your child early. Start this pattern as soon as possible because it will be tougher as your child becomes older. There is nothing wrong with nap-time. Give your kids a set nap-time if they are pre-school aged and younger. Along with that set a bedtime! The recommended amount of hours for kids is at least 8 hours. One way to create this calculation is to subtract 8 hours plus morning preparation time from the time they should be at school.

For instance if it takes 1 hour of morning preparation plus 30 minutes to get to school at 7:00am

7:00am - 8 hours (sleep) + 1 hour (morning prep) + 30 minutes (Commute) = 8:30pm

As you can see from the equation above, this child should be in bed by 8:30pm.

I have personally seen little kindergartners who could not function properly in one of the most interactive and responsive classrooms, because they were not given a sleep routine at home. I have worked with kids who are very capable of achieving high standards but simply cannot because they are so sleepy that they cannot think straight. Please do your child, yourself, and their school a favor by developing a sleep routine for your child.

Chapter 13: Motivation

Motivation is directed by the desires and actions of people and their desires or needs. Typically kids have desires and as a parent you need to simulate them in order to accomplish his or her goals and desires.

IMPACTS OF MOTIVATION TO KIDS

Motivation is what drives a child to change behaviour and habits. Motivation models a child to achieve goals and targets. It is a setup to start learning vast skills and behaviour.

Infants have tender brain and thus at their tender age the kids learn by capturing ideas by studying faces and voices together with actions. The kids will therefore find themselves social to people with voices and different faces. Motivating a young kid can be by buying your kid a toy making some sounds which he or she loves if he or she achieves something you trained him or her to work on it.

Kids will grow knowing what to do to achieve a token of appreciation from the parent and as many parents would want to grow a disciplined kid, the parent also need some things to do in order to make a kid aspire for a motivation from you;

Learning habits

Young infants need to be learned when tender. When an infant is young, you will note that you will give your kid something, he or she will look at it and move his or her face away in despair and seem to get bored. These are some habitual learning a parent has to note while the child is still young and upon getting old you will have known a better way to motivate your kid.

Motivate using play

Research has it that kids learn more when they play. This not only is a form of refreshment but also a form of physical activity that will make the kid physically fit.

Carefully observe the children play expression upon introducing a game to him or her. Parents might need to transform their homes to playground by introducing swings and maybe buying a ball since scientifically it's proven that boys like soccer. Ideally, girls like rope skipping and colourful games.

Parents will note great improve in children behaviour and especially child growth physically and mentally. Also parents would note classroom improvement.

HOW TO MOTIVATE YOUR CHILDREN

Motivating children is simple. Once the parent gets habitual learning of the kid, motivation come by its way. Taking interest of a kid is good and will help the parent identify a mode of motivation to the child. Toddlers have many interests. Some may like playing video games while others will like singing, dancing, playing soccer and much more. This is a great chance to the parent to identify a mode of motivation. All you need is simple. Set a goal to the kid and tell him or her that once he or she achieves the goal, you buy him a play station or a soccer ball or a guitar and much other gifts depending on the kid's interest. The kid will struggle to achieve the set goal.

As a parent, you also need to guide the child on how to achieve the set goal. Set out simple steps for the kid to follow. List them and display somewhere to sound like a reminder. You will be shocked that the kid might engage in some illegal things just in order to grab that 'guitar' you had promised him. For example, when you set a goal for your kid to attain certain grade and buy him something, the kid might engage in exam irregularity just for him or her to get what he or she had been promised. So parents need to keep watch at their children if they are following the set steps you had for him or her.

When a runner is in the track, his fans cheer him by shouting at him to increase pace since the race is so competitive. Ideally, make your child know the world is competitive. Always note his or her classwork progress and cheer him or her up in order to make him excel in classwork.

Make an effort to make a celebration once your child accomplishes a task you had given him or her.

Negative motivators are disliked by many guardians and parents. This would absolutely work perfect to your kid but if and only if used sparingly since it might lead to a kid losing power. For the negative motivation to be more effective, your kid needs to be so clear in following rules and note the consequences aligned to breaking rules.

Apparently, discipline doesn't come by force and being a strict parent. Discipline comes from the insight of love and concern for the safety and especially well being.

Model him or her to have a calm behaviour. Kids throwing insults when angry and frustrated are growing in number nowadays. For the parent, they should teach kids that being angry and throwing insults can be avoided and mere frustrations can be cured by just simple and calm ways rather acting strange. Engaging with your shouting kid is not bad but you need to take a greater step as a parent. Training your kid to apologize will help so much. Let the kid stay calm after getting mad, and slowly teach him or her to learn how to apologize when angry or frustrated

Understand are children the way they are. Some kids are hard and some might not only be because of their behaviour but also it is proven scientifically that some traits are inherited and are observed from the children which when trying to get to a scope of it, you will learn that some of your people in your lineage has the similar traits to your kid and you should not blame the child but understand the kid the way he or she is.

Chapter 14: What You Need To Teach Your Daughter

As a parent, you likely want to support your daughter and give her all the advice she needs before she tells you she is ready to face the world. Before she even turns ten years old, you will feel more aware of her transformation from a little girl to a teenager.

By this time you are probably thinking of the things that you want your daughter to know about. Remember that she is her own person, so the best you can do to make your daughter understand is to just love them. Do not try to force her to take dancing lessons, or to bake, or to throw a ball. She should not be made to feel that she is forced to do something

The advice you give to your daughter should be something that she can actually use and ponder on as she grows older, and when she finally becomes an adult. Here are a couple of things you can consider for your list:

**Tell her that she is valuable. Remember that it is important that your daughter knows and understands that she is extremely valued and important to you, and that you will protect her. Explain that you may have to set boundaries and rules because you love her. With these rules, she will find comfort and safety, even if she decides to push against them.

**Teach your daughter to never be afraid to express herself and share her passion with others. For example, she may find it hard to tell her friends that she still plays with dolls, and she might worry that she will be made fun of for it. Teach her that friends who tease you for the things you love are not true friends. Although this is hard to realize, this is an essential lesson that your daughter needs to learn. Peer pressure is one of the toughest hurdles teenagers go through and letting her how know she can cope would be helpful.

**Your daughter needs to know that you are proud of her and she is enough for you. Always tell her that you will always choose her out of all the girls in the world. Never forget to build your daughter's esteem by telling her how beautiful she is. Never compare her to others. Although she will be tempted to spend a large amount of time in her life trying to prove to herself that she has something of value, you can create an atmosphere where she will be loved.

**Let her know that it is important that she take care of herself. As a woman, it is very easy to put the needs of others on top of your own. It can even be necessity, sometimes, and it can also be a developed habit. Tell your daughter to never neglect her own needs. If she is tired, she must learn to give herself rest and sleep. If she feels that she needs some time alone, then make her understand that it is perfectly fine for her to feel that way and to do what she wants to attain it. Make her understand that it is beautiful that she cares about people but that she does not need to take care of everything all the time.

**In connection to this, teach your daughter to never feel bad about spending money on what she loves. This will be an essential key to make herself happy in the future. However, tell her that this does not mean that she should max out her credit card, or spend every single cent that she will have. Simply teach her that if she needs a small indulgence or reward, it is okay to give in to it.

**Teach her not to blame herself for the problems of her friends. As she goes on in her life she will encounter problems and mean girls, as well as the pressures in her world which will hurt and bring her down. She will need to hear the opposite from you at home. Help her understand that when her friends act in a manner which hurts her and makes her feel insecure for some reason, it has something to do with what goes on inside them, and not with her.

Chapter 15: The Arrival Of The Children

It is important to initiate conversations with your kids, especially if they are boys. It's good to pay detailed attention to them, as one does to his work and investments. As human beings, they are of no less importance.

Be proud that you have unleashed these agents of light to the world during your earthly journey. Be a progenitor of good kids, whether they are your biological children or adopted. If the children came through your loins as a mistake, it does not really matter. Do not sulk. Do not regret. Ask for assistance. Do not throw them away, physically or mentally. Reflect on my previous words. You won't be here again.

You have become a part-creator with the Great but unseen Divine, that is love. So show love to your kids but don't spoil them with unbalanced affection, which is not reality!

Children as the third leg of the tripod come in, to make a family unit and this not due to their own prior making. Proper planning, towards nurturing them into adulthood must be in place. This is with the aim so that they can be useful to themselves and others; children that parents would be proud of. Children as the citizens, that the larger society and beyond could be accorded respect.

However, achieving these results demand a lot of work, from mums and dads. More so, when boys are the children we are contending with.
Bringing up of children of different genders, require different approaches and strategies. Many women have to contend with a lot to nurture young boys into responsible young men.

There are little tricks boys can play with their mum and not with their father. And same, girls do to ignorant fathers. This is why it tends to be natural, for dads and mums to be there, to nurture that innocent and naive baby, into a cognitive balanced individual in the society. It is not in many cases that single parenthood succeeds in bringing up balanced children. And it's not in all cases where the presence of the father and mother figure would guarantee absolute success.

As I write this, my two children are relatively young men, the senior one is about 28 years of age while the younger one, is about 25 years old. We currently reside in Africa but in today's era of globalization, they are not immune to the trending but confusing global culture. These are influential times that are quite confusing, for young people who are inundated with so much information. Many pre-teenage kids cannot even filter the barrage of information, without the guidance of well informed but good intentioned adults.

Though yet unmarried and having attained their own relative independence from me as a dad, I still chip in a few words of smart advice occasionally, to my children, even as young adults. Lately, I deliberately do less of this prodding because they have attained that lofty behavioral personality today, as I envisaged, when they were still infants. They are not robotic in their manners. They are self-opinionated. Definitely they have done well for themselves. They may not behave exactly as one desires or like their parents, but my wife and I have nurtured them, so that they can hold their own in many circumstances.

I can choose to close my eyes, to a large extent that they will not be a disappointment. I don't wish them to derail from being good citizens. I am rest assured; I have done my long bit of sacrificing and with the huge support of my wife - being their guide and guards. As they say, the rest is now up to them. And this, I do tell them.

One has to be realistic about the nature of Man. Parents must be realistic, about unforeseen challenges. Since experience is the best teacher, one may not know how the kids would handle some situations, as they progress through their life journeys. But if parents or guardians have played their part, the challenges are easier to tackle by the children, when they become of age. We will not always be with them.

Nurturing My Boys, From Cradle To Adulthood

Talking about boys and for me as a dad, I knew it was not going to be easy to bring boys up to maturity and decency especially in the present world. A world where there are so many shifting but warped values. Some of these confusing values find more increasing channels to reach and influence everybody; the privacy and innocent minds of young people are not excluded.

So a wise parent would ask, "How can I lead my children through all these?" Therefore, parenting is becoming tougher for modern parents. Meeting the objectives of raising well behaved young adults in my own case had the aforementioned at the back of my mind. Now, how did I, as a man, achieve the modest success of up-bringring of the two gentlemen, the society can be proud of?

When I newly got married, I quickly discovered that my wife was an easy going woman. I was not sure I could leave the direct upbringing of the boys to her alone. I had to be decisive with the boys, I also realized.

At my own relatively young age as a dad, I knew boys would draw rings around my wife.d

It came to my notice that many women

were not succesful raising boys. Some single mothers had a rather fatal and heart rending experience, eventually. As kids traverse the teenage years, characters would have been set. And it had better be of a positive slant before it is too late.
I had seen many sad examples of difficult children and I cringe. I cringe of the pains these young adults bring to themselves and the family. So I made up my mind that I wouldn't let this happen to me, more so if they were boys. I needed to be subtle and firm but close to them, right from their innocent years. A bond must be established between me and my boys. Since marriage was a venture I had bought into, I told myself it must give me good returns.

Good returns of everything that it entails. That will include bringing up well-behaved children.

I realized you couldn't take it for granted or take chances with these innocent but inquisitive souls. If one is not ready to do the hard job of parenting which takes many years, then, do not bring kids to the world! Otherwise it might be regrettable. And I did not want to be a loser for lack of tact and dedication to my boys. I am relieved today because in the recent years, they have been making some positive initiatives.

I can have my own independence today, giving more attention to my wife, my work, self and other people that I share moments with. So I knew I had to strain to do the work of balancing my work, nurturing the children in the presence of my other activities. The woman cannot do it all. I told myself, being boys; it will be a little bit more challenging to influence them without my male physical presence.

At every opportunity I had to be in their presence, I ensured that took place. Even as infants, I engaged them in constant

interaction. Though initially, it tended to be a series of monologue from me but by the time they clocked 4years of age, I encouraged them to tell me how they felt about things.
I started studying the personality of each one from the first year birthday. No two children are the same. From what I gathered, there are subtle differences even in the mannerism of identical twins. I ensured constant rapport. I washed them at bath, even as they routinely complained to their mum that my scrubbing was too hard. I washed their teeth hard. But I left the cleaning-up after toileting, to my wife. She was ok with that. I wasn't. Ah ha! In-fact to remove the fear of mathematics, that is still a common issue amongst the youths, I took it upon myself to give them additional lessons at home. Rather than use the abstract approach, to teach elementary arithmetic fraction, I used oranges to illustrate that concept. And we all sucked the oranges afterwards. Both of

them never got threatened by mathematic stuff, even in their university years.

At the tender age, it was also fun to do a spontaneous karaoke, without the music box and mike. Our popular song was the Whitney Houston's song "Greatest Love of All". We enjoyed singing it very well, even though we struggled with the incomplete lyrics.

I had my fair share of aping the WWA, the American wrestling series. I tried a few stupid moves with them on the carpet and thereafter left the two of them to it, when I got tired. I allowed to be beaten each time. A pity there was not an immediate recording device, like a smart phone then. Today, they seem not to remember these plays, when reminded.
I guess at their coming of age, they don't want to be reminded of those "childish phases".

I understand. They pretend it didn't happen. Maybe they have forgotten or pretending they can't recall. You know children do have their own mind. I don't bother to probe further. Though, their mum does tease them about their childish past, once in a while.

Chapter 16: Child Parenting Methods

Parenting children involves some identifiable methods in our ancient and modern family settings. In some homes, authoritative style, authoritarian style, permissive style and uninvolved style of parenting are enforced.

Notably, authoritative parents are more aware of the children feelings and capabilities and they support their efforts. The parents usually allow some reasonable limited autonomy to the children and there is always a balance of give-and-take or "win –win," situation or atmosphere in communication between the parents and the children.

In the case of authoritarian style of parenting, the parents are extremely strict and rigid in the way and manner of their children respond to the rules and orders in their home. The parents strictly enforce obedience and moral behavior on their kids. This authoritarian style of parenting is common among the working-class and middle-class parents who try to mold a certain pattern of behavior on their children. However, children raised in an authoritarian style of parenting tend to be passive, hostile and even rebellious at the end.

The next is, permissive parenting setting. In this case, parents allow some reasonable and responsible freedom to their children. Most of the time, the parents rely mostly on reasoning and explanations from the kids. Consequently, it is believed that children from a permissive parenting style tend to be generally happier than kids from the other parenting styles.

Nevertheless, it is also believed that the children from permissive parenting setting sometimes show low levels of self-control and self-reliance. This is caused as a result of lack of certain structures and certain rules at home. Most middle-class parents use permissive parenting method in rearing their children.

However, some parents practice a style of parenting known as, "Uninvolved parenting," in which the children are left without adequate attention or concern from the parents. The parents don't bother to talk to the kids regarding "Rights and Wrongs," thereby exposing them to moral decadents. The normal parents-children relationship is totally absent in an uninvolved parenting setting. The kids are allowed to behave anyhow and any way and the parents are careless about their behavior or outcome of their actions.

Although, there is no absolute perfect and definitive parenting style, most parents try to integrate authoritative, authoritarian and permissive parenting styles to strike a balance in parenting their children. Parents in the modern settings try to communicate with the kids as often as time allows them both verbally and non-verbally. With that, the children future and behavior will be well fashioned and planned. The modern day technology has made it even much easier for parents.

Neither authoritarian nor permissive parenting is loving parenting. Loving parenting is parenting that values both the parents' and the children's feelings and needs. Loving parents do not attempt to control their children other than in actual situations of health and safety, nor do they allow their children to control them. They do not violate their children with anger, blame, or hitting, nor do they allow their children to violate them. They do not expect their children to give up themselves for them, nor do they give themselves up for their children.

Loving parents are parents who deeply value themselves enough to not worry about being rejected by their children. They are willing to set solid limits on unacceptable behavior and are not available to being manipulated by the children. Their identities are not tied into their children's performance in school or in other activities, such as sports. Nor are their identities tied up in how their children look. They are accepting of who their children are as individuals, even when their children are very different from them. They do not impose their way of being onto their children, yet at the same time they solidly reinforce a value system that includes honesty, integrity, caring, compassion, kindness and empathy.

As much as we want to be loving parents, unless we have done our own inner work to heal our own deep fears of rejection and domination, we will automatically be acting out of these fears without being consciously aware of it. If you grew up with fears of rejection and/or domination, you will automatically protect against these fears in your relationships with your children. You may find yourself trying to control them out of a fear of being controlled or rejected by them. You might be controlling with your anger or with your giving in and giving yourself up.

Fears of rejection can manifest with children through trying to control them with anger, or through trying to control their love through giving yourself up to them. Fears of domination can manifest through controlling them with anger or violence to avoid being controlled by them. Insecurities can manifest through attempting to get your children to perform in the way you want in order to define your worth. Perhaps, it is time to accept that we need to be in the process of healing ourselves before becoming parents.

In one way or another, whatever is unhealed within you will surface in your behavior with your children. Raising healthy children means first healing the wounded child within you and the part of you that has your fears and insecurities, your desire to protect against rejection and domination.

Our society has swung back and forth between authoritarian and permissive parenting and the result of both is far less than desirable. We have only to look at the number of people taking antidepressants and anti-anxiety drugs, as well as the number of alcoholics and drug addicts, as well as the rise of crime and the number of people in prisons, to know that neither method works to raise healthy individuals.

Chapter 17: How To Talk To Your Child About Molestation

Talking to children about this topic can be very difficult for most parents. How can you warn your child about some potential dangers without discrediting their natural trust of people or destroying their view that we are living in a good world? As such, it might seem logical to shy away from this topic because you think there are no objective ways to discuss the negative notions of sexuality like children exploitation by adults without portraying disapproval on healthy physical affection. Nevertheless, the media is constantly bombarding the headlines with stories and events involving burglaries, murders, rapes, kidnappings and molestations. You need to help put these events into perspective by helping your children interpret these events. You need to discus about some of the precautions they can take to evade a potential molester. No one is safe when it comes to child molestation. It can occur in any neighborhood. The molester can be of any race, age or economic level. In fact, most of the times, the molester is someone we know. It could be a family acquaintance or a relative. The victim can be male or female. As such, to help them protect themselves, you could use some of these suggestions:

Teach your child their addresses, full names, and phone numbers, and let them know your work place and your neighbors' phone numbers. Be sure that they also know how to use the 911 emergency numbers.

Discuss with them about their bodies, including the penis, vagina and breasts. Let them know that these parts are private and ought to remain that way.

Be proactive by telling them to let you, a guardian or teacher know if anyone tries to look, touch their private parts, take pictures of their private parts or show them images of private parts.

Teach them to also tell you if someone (an adult) tells them to keep a secret. Let them know that these kinds of secrets are not allowed.

Talk to them of the tactics used by people who want to molest them such as giving them gifts or candy, or threatening them with scare tactics like separating them from their family or giving them punishment. Let them know that this is wrong and that those who engage in this behavior will get in trouble.

Give them specific ideas of what to watch out for and the permission to say no and make their leave when they feel a situation is uncomfortable. You should communicate any strange incidents that take place in your neighborhood, childcare setting, school or even in the family to the appropriate authority be it the police, school principle, your physician, or director. This information should be shared among the members of your community, through either, phone trees, fliers or online groups as a way of safety mobilization. Be sure to safeguard the privacy of the family involved. The issue of child molestation is very delicate, and as such should be approached with caution. Programs about child abuse prevention also need to tread carefully when they approach this topic. You should be forewarn when such a program is being conducted in your child's school classroom or childcare. Examine the approach and materials being used, and research the background of the persons involved.

The tips discussed are merely the beginning. The way you talk to your child when such a scenario occurs needs all your skills and wisdom as a parent. Your initial response when something happens in your family is especially important. It is vital that you remain as calm as possible to avoid rubbing your own sense of horror and panic on your child. The first thing you should do is to spend the time to get the specifics and reassure your child as best as you can. Avoid leading questions and let them explain in their own way what happened. Should you find yourself in this dilemma, you can find comfort in some community organizations that could help you.

Generally, positive social relationships are important for everyone's well being. Your child should be surrounded with close and supportive friends and family. Developing good teenage friendships must root from good parent and child relationships. In addition, it also helps with self-esteem when you teach your child the value of doing good to others. There are various ways that your child could help the family or friends such as giving up a seat on the bus, or giving someone a hand when they have dropped some papers in the streets. They could also get involved in community activity. Similarly, when they learn how to take care of themselves physically, emotionally and mentally, it can help boost their self-esteem. It is important to get active, take a break from technology, go outside and make sure that they get enough sleep as this can greatly improve their mood as well as their physical fitness.

Chapter 18: Childproofing Your Rv

Parents who are accustomed to travelling with babies in conventional vehicles know the importance of safety belts and booster seats. However, when it comes to travelling with an RV, traditional methods of restraint and legal requirements can become drastically different. RV's are efficient vehicles for travelling on long distances and provide excellent space for children to be entertained; it also allows more room for risk and can lead to potential accidents if parents are prepared. The range of style classes available for RV's is incredibly versatile these days, which makes it important for guardians to familiarize themselves with their own model, and how to best make it child-proof for babies and toddlers alike.

The often spread message of larger vehicles being able to withstand high impact crashes is true in many aspects, however it should not justify poorly managing the arrangement of an RV vehicle. This claim can lull parents into a false sense of security, particularly if they compare structural standards to similar large-sized vehicles like buses. These standards should be individually reviewed and analyzed, as each model features different architecture and design choices that dictate the overall vitality and sturdiness of a given vehicle.

For example, when it comes to installing booster seats or car seats, they should not be implemented on side-facing or rearward positions. This may result in life-threatening injuries for babies or children fitted into these customizations. Other potential threats include the prospect of loose-flying objects occurring in the event of a crash, even 'built-in' applications like cupboards are susceptible to becoming loose during a crash, so extra care and skepticism should be applied when enforcing safety measures for your children.

Other important questions need to be asked when planning an RV trip. Which toys should you bring from home for the RV and other entertainment suggestions should be considered during the initial process. Caregivers can avoid the risk of children roaming inside the RV during travel, by providing leisurely options that allow for seating arrangements that don't restrict play time. Driving an RV through unpredictable terrain can result in sudden bumps and jumps, babies and other children should be restrained for the majority duration of the trip to ensure maximum safety.

Travel arrangements need to be considered prior to taking off. In the event of towing an external passenger vehicle with your RV, try to arrange a secondary driver to operate the vehicle separately, where children will be more comfortable than an RV setting.

If this option is not possible, taken extensive measures to secure seating arrangements that are most comfortable for travelling children. Having a baby sit up-front in the passenger seat is the safest option for parents, as the structural integrity of most RV's is best preserved in the cockpit area.

In regards to entertainment, which toys should you bring from home for the RV, is an important part of the preparation process. With the advancement of technology making portable gaming a viable option for children, small entertainment devices provide a perfect distraction for kids to interact and learn without the necessity for constant supervision. Books and quality reading material is also a great opportunity to delve into fictional worlds, along with fun educational reading that can involve parents in the learning process too.

The major downside to these options is the potential for car sickness to occur, suitable medication exists to alleviate these common symptoms of long road trips, however this may not be suitable for infants. Regardless of what entertainment options parents decide upon for their road trip, careful planning and proper measures should be implemented to ensure a satisfying and stress-free trip for both children and caregivers alike.

Taking regular stops is a vital aspect of breaking up the trip. This allows people to relax, unwind and stretch their muscles after spending hours in a confined vehicle. When planning an extensive trip, seek out local restaurants, landmarks and other points-of-interest so that children will have the opportunity to unwind. Restaurants and eateries are commonplace in regional areas (as long as you plan accordingly) and provide great entertainment for kids, along with replenishing vital energy and filling empty stomachs.

Landmarks such as parks, gift shops or petrol stations, no matter how glamorous, can provide relief from long trips. Souvenir shops allow children and caregivers to collect little memorabilia, which serves as an important reminder of the time spent together and the journey ahead. Petrol stations allow for basic vehicle maintenance tasks to be done, ensuring consistent fluid levels including oil, coolant and fuel top-ups. Researching the areas and vicinities that will be passed during a road trip will ensure vital pit-stops are taken at regular intervals, this will guarantee a more pleasant adventure for all participants involved.

The duration of a trip will dictate the placement of important furniture and nursing areas for children whilst the RV is being driven. A workable arrangement is possible with proper planning and understanding of a vehicle's structural limitations. Minimalist approaches such as collapsible travel beds and smaller sized cribs are perfectly viable options for parents. The occupied space of a changing table can be avoided by incorporating a changing pad on the bed; non-essential furnishings such as dressers can be avoided by utilizing built-in drawers or cabinets available in the RV unit.

When it comes to planning and preparing a family trip across the state, take into consideration the restrictions and structural integrity of a given vehicle. Avoid rear or side-facing seats and install only forward-facing seats for all passengers. Maintain a guide to local areas of interests and available restaurants, in order to have breaks during the long drive

With enough preparation in-place for caregivers to provide for their children, a fun and enjoyable road trip can be successfully executed that benefits the whole family, that way, all members will have fond memories of the precious time spent together.

Chapter 19: Helping The Child To Overcome His Sensory Problems

When your son or your daughter has problems with a noisy neighbourhood and hence fears to get out and go to play like the other kids, then you probably would be disappointed that, he or she is not like the other kids. It is understandable that you wish for your child to be like the others and play like the others or in simple terms is very 'normal' in his behaviour. But, what you also need to pay attention to is that, these sensory signals are not your child's choice, but a condition that he has to live with, for no fault of his own. Though parenting him may require additional thought and bring upon a different challenge every day, with enough determination on your part, you will be able to reduce the discomfort of your child to a bare minimum and also make their behaviour much more socially acceptable.

Knowing what is right for your son may not be easy, as it might require a thorough research of the situation and the perusal of a number of writings on the subject. But, you should remember that, at the end of it all, you will see a more refined behaviour in your kid. Most of the kids with sensory problems are not aware of the societal demands from them. They tend to live within their own space and yield for their own needs. This can be anything from having an urge to talk incessantly or having no interest to communicate with the other at all. This is how varied the situations are. Every child has a unique condition and hence requires different approaches.

Owing to the fact that there is a huge list of conditions, out of which your child could have one or more, you will need to be very well-equipped in dealing with all of these conditions effectively. Reading books like these will give you a general understanding of each of the situations, enabling you to expect certain acts and behaviours of your child. However, it is also true that the suggested methods will work to different extents on each of the kids. This is because; every child receives inputs in a different manner and responds to them in a different way. So, if another kid with the same condition shows better response to a specific type of treatment method, then there is nothing to be afraid of. This does not mean that your kid's condition is much worse than the former's. Instead, it only means that your child needs more time processing the information and then acting on it.

As long as he is showing some signs of progress, you will have nothing to worry about. The problem arises when he shows no development at all. 1in such cases, you will need to test your method in dealing with his situation. Even if after long durations of being in practice it does seem to have any visible effects, then you should consider revising it, improving on it or replacing it altogether. Every strategy needs to be very smart and innovative and appeal to your kid. Only then will he show some amount of interest in it. If you ask a child who loves to collect butterflies and bugs to suddenly turn to music and dance, he is less likely to do so. On the other hand, if you want him to stay safe and little less obsessed with bugs, then you could bring him books and pictures of different bugs that will keep him occupied and hence cut down the amount of time he spends on finding bugs around the house.

On the other hand, if your child hates to travel in the school bus on account of the extraordinary clatter and commotion that inhibits it, then you could get ear plugs for your kid and that way reduce the impact of the noise on him. You could also try and get him acquainted with these situations little by little, so that he knows how to not react in the face of them. However, you need to be very patient in these cases and not expect drastic changes. Every little improvement that may seem minute for us will be very huge and require a lot of effort from his side.

If your child who cannot bear the experience of tight fitted and itchy clothes manages to adorn a formal suit for hours together, then that is s huge accomplishment on his part and you will need to give him his due credits for the same. Little appraisals like this after every little development gives these children an encouraging nod to continue in the same direction, even if it requires a lot of efforts from their side.

Knowing what your child needs, when and how much is important. Because, your child may not be in the habit of asking for the things he likes, like other children, he will just like to do or have it. If you could teach him to communicate his needs, then he would be better off even in your absence. However, if it is otherwise, you always will need to keep track of when your child feels comfortable eating or sleeping, because certain kids will need to have a precise schedule for it all. Understanding your kid's needs is the first step in helping him to overcome his condition and you will have to do this with care and precision.

Chapter 20: A Confident Teen Is Less Trouble

The root reason teenagers seek out and participate in risky behaviors is that they desire to be accepted as part of something bigger than themselves.

If you can involve your teen in an extracurricular activity it often meets their need to belong to a group with a common interest. No one has to feel different because they all wear the same uniform – so to speak.

There are all kinds of clubs teens can belong to. Ski clubs, swimming clubs, band, and especially sports teams at school.

The rule I had for my teens was, "You're going to be somewhere doing something, or you're going to be home".

One of the advantages of school activities is that there is adult supervision built in.

Look for healthy, adult supervised groups for you child to join.

You'll likely find that the supervision factor alone will lighten your load to some degree.

Whether your teen is involved in music, sports or volunteer opportunities you will find that such activities will not only benefit your teenager in the short term, but the long term as well.

Building character, healthy body's and providing appropriate social interactions is all part of developing self worth in young people.

The confidence that comes with achievement is priceless. The effort it takes to achieve, even small feats, builds self worth, and self worth builds confidence, and confidence helps youngsters become leaders instead of followers.

Not all students are academically gifted, but opportunities for meeting goals, working as a team member and learning to persevere are offered in a variety of other venues.

Parents must start early in helping their child find that healthy place of belonging, beyond the family, whereby their child can excel. Such experiences are vital to the social development of children.

Furthermore, having another entity for the child to be accountable to will benefit even the parents in the long run. I am a firm believer that it takes a village to raise a child.

Defusing the Violent or Aggressive Teen

This chapter is not applicable to every parent who purchases this booklet. However, you may wish to read the chapter for your own information, or you may know a parent this chapter would greatly benefit. Either way, I am including the chapter for informational purposes only and it is not intended to have stand alone therapeutic value.

One of the first things a parent needs to do if they have an aggressive teen is put a stop to the behavior. In some cases the child has learned the behavior from the parent, so taking a look at your own methods for handling frustration and anger may be your first step.

I worked as a counselor at a residential center for teens for many years. I have personally witnessed instances where professionals deliberately escalated teens' frustration to the point of aggression. I do not recommend a parent do that. I can't recall a single time there was an appreciable benefit to that technique.

If you cannot carry out a discussion calmly with your teenager then you need to bring in outside counsel. I like to think of counseling as parent – teen coaching. Like other coaching, it takes time and hard work to achieve a goal, but if the players stick together they can do it.

The following steps may seem extreme and harsh, but if you have an aggressive teenager the cold hard facts are that you're in a zone that has moved beyond civilized behavior. I suggest you close this book if you're not prepared to face up to that fact.

Know the Law:

·Everyone in the house needs to realize that domestic violence is no longer tolerated in most jurisdictions within the United States, and as such is a jailable offence.

·Even making someone fear for their safety is considered fourth degree assault in most states.

·It is against the law to interrupt the reporting of a crime.

·It is against the law to falsely report a crime.

Call a family meeting and announce that the aggression has stopped – period. Ask for suggestions of how the family should express their anger or frustrations?

Take even the youngest child's suggestions and write them down. The feelings of everyone in the family need to be acknowledged. You may even want to make a written, Declaration of Peace and have everyone sign it.

The one thing that is the most vital is that everyone agrees there will be no more violence or aggression in your home. Everyone has permission to walk outside to take a time out, but let it be known that where ever and whenever the discussion is taking place the meeting will continue once they return.

Whether or not family meetings lasts until midnight is not important. Meeting the goal that your family will work together to design a plan for dealing with anger and frustrations in a civilized manner is vital.

Tell your teens that the faster you get through the main points (don't try to resolve every little issue at one sitting) the faster the meeting ends. Don't hesitate to use time outs.

Even professional sports teams use "Time Outs" to run the clock out. Use the clock to your advantage to produce fatigue, boredom, and help people realize just how petty some of their complaints really are.

Suggestions You May Want to Try:

1. If you can't talk without yelling at each other then text your feelings to each other

2. Have each person make a list of their grievances

3. Once the meeting begins you may want to ask everyone to hold off on 2 or 3 things from their list for future discussions

4. Allow each person to read their list of grievances – be sure to stay calm

5. You may need to invite a respected friend or family member over to act as the chairperson

6. Use parliamentary procedure to add a sense of security, humor, and equality to your meetings

7. Vote for solutions when possible

8. Hold your meeting in a public place where people are forced to behave

9. Always end serious meetings with a fun event or reward that the whole family will stick around for

10. NEVER, EVER ambush your family! Always let them know the 3 W's. What will be discussed, When and Where the meetings will take place

11. Give up on the idea that this is a "private" family matter – if the cops get called due to an assault it will be in the local paper under police reports anyway.

The purpose of your meeting is to avert that if at all possible.

Going forward, the family bylaws need to state that the police will be called if an aggressive or violent eruption occurs in your home again. Just be sure it's made clear that jail time will be the likely outcome for the offender.

You should further explain that once the police are called there is no point in running because they will simply issue an arrest warrant.

Everyone needs to hang tight so they can tell their side of the story. Officers are trained to sort out the details and can often leave the scene with no one in custody.

Chapter 21: Kids need someone to talk

Be there. This is such a simple little thing. Just being around and available for when they need you for something or just a person to talk to. Kids need someone to talk to when the world gets confusing and scary. Sometimes it may take time for them to find someone to talk to, or even to be ready to talk. Often the moment they're willing to open up is fleeting. The important thing is to be around when they need you. Being available can be hard. There's stuff to do, dinner to put on the table and bills to pay. It isn't easy to be available with a full-time job. It isn't easy to show up to school events, plays, recitals, get the right kids to the right lessons and still take care of the things that need to be taken care of.

This goes hand in hand with being open and honest with your children as discussed above. Like all other things, it's impossible to be available to discuss day to day struggles on a constant basis. There are still responsibilities that have to be done, but try to squeeze in what kind of time that you can do. Try to take a couple extra minutes to stop focusing on the phone and start focusing on what they're saying. They'll thank you for it later in life.

Everyone has had that problem that was difficult to discuss. Those problems get a lot easier to talk about if someone you trust is available to talk to. Listen. Children will speak their mind, sometimes it may be hidden, or they may not have the right words to explain what's going on. For that, active listening is a good way to go.

Active listening is a process, it involves asking probing questions to get long-form answers and actually paying attention to not only what's being said, but how it's being said. Kids communicate in many different ways. I've become well versed in the language of slamming doors and rolling eyes over the years, and I would hazard a guess that just about any other parent out there is just as good at that language as I am. Kids say things without saying the words. If they're frustrated or scared, they react, sometimes non-verbally. It's the same with anyone, but kids are just learning how to communicate, so it gets harder for them to even understand their own feelings, much less tell someone how they feel.

This is why it's so important for a parent to be there for them. Be available as much as possible, present themselves as someone that they can talk to. A good way to do that is to communicate with them. Talk to them about things. It's easy to want to shelter children from all of the painful parts of life, but they're going to have to face it, so learn a language that they can understand and is something that is appropriate and open the lines of communication.

In no way does this mean that it's alright to just dump all your problems and worries on them, but if money is tight, talk to them, come up with a plan to work it out as a family. You may be surprised at the kind of insight that a child can come up with to help. Trust them and you'll be surprised at how the trust can grow between a parent and child.

Keep in mind that it is easy to be uncomfortably open in any situation. A child is not someone that you can pile frustration after frustration on, but instead talk to them about situations that may change their lives. A family friend going through a divorce or death of a member of the family are examples of painful things that affect everyone. Talking to a child about how to handle the death, instead of hiding things and hoping that they don't know.

Chapter 22: Challenges 3 And 4 - Changes In Your Lifestyle And Relationship

Having a child changes your lifestyle and relationship in several ways. Beyond the new responsibilities of putting your children first, you also have to cut back on certain things you do and conserve the money you make.

Here are a few of the changes your lifestyle may experience:

Fewer nights out

Lack of sleep/consistent sleep

Monetary changes

Less sex

Increased worries

A few of the changes listed are going to continually be repeated because they are not only changes in your lifestyle, but also emotional and relationship changes based on the new responsibilities you have.

Putting your children first, requires spending money on them and not yourself. Yes, it would be great to spend $500 on new race car seats in your sports car, but that $500 might be needed for the diapers, food, and clothing your child or children need. It does depend on your income and your expenses, but the point being made is—you may need to adjust your expenditures to cover the new costs and the savings you should start for your child/children.

Monetarily and for the benefit of your children, going out each night is not an option. Taking time for yourself when they are in school or one night a week is beneficial, but every night is putting yourself first.

Your sleep changes the instant you bring home a baby. For a few years, you will need to get up in the middle of the night to attend to their needs. These needs are feeding and diaper changes at first. As your child becomes two or three, nightmares can begin. Dealing with a scared child or a sick child in the night changes your sleep patterns.

Due to a lack of sleep or interruptions your sex life is going to change. If you have one child, you may find after a few months, when your baby is able to sleep longer, you will be able to get back to a regular, enjoyable sex life. After two children, depending on how close in age they are, you may find your sex life is changed again, with less frequency to enjoy such a pleasure. You certainly have to be more careful, when your children are walking age that they are unable to see you enjoying sex.

Part of the sleep interruption can also be more worries. You might have concerns about money, about your child, or if you are raising your child correctly. These worries are normal, but it can lead to changes in your lifestyle. You will definitely child proof your home, and perhaps stop buying certain things because you don't want your child to get into it.

Parenting is going to be about making sacrifices and choices that will adapt your lifestyle.

Changes in Your Relationship

Sex is certainly one change in your relationship that occurs. However, there will be other changes. It is not just the two of you anymore. There is at least one other person to think about.

Negative emotions and lack of sleep are two things that can impact your relationship. For example, if one parent seems better able to handle the change in lifestyle and responsibilities than another—jealousy can rise.

Being extremely tired can cause heightened emotions, which can lay the ground for arguments. Words such as "you never think of me anymore, you never buy me flowers, or you are leaving all the responsibility of the child to me…" are harmful and happen.

The key is to always have time for yourselves together without your children, as well as have time for yourself on your own.

Remember when you first started dating and you wanted to spend every waking minute together? You eventually adapted to spending time on your hobbies and the other person on their hobbies.

When you chose to get married or live together, you adjusted to ensure you both were not feeling smothered. You are going to need to make some changes again. This time it is about taking the time to have a night out as a couple or a night in. You will also need to set aside time when you both have free time on your own to follow your hobbies.

For example, if you love to read, you might take a book, go to a coffee shop, library, or some park and read for an hour. Your child or children will be with your spouse or significant other. Another day or that same day, your partner may go out for an hour to do something they enjoy.

By making the effort to spend time doing things you enjoy, separately and as a couple, you will be able to keep your relationship healthy. Parents who do not do these things will have more significant changes to their relationship.

Your relationship can sour or you may start to think about divorce. Accept that some changes will happen, and do your best to keep time for each other and yourself.

Coping with Changes

It is an adjustment. You have committed to having a child. As the parent, you have to realize you are changing your life and adapt to it the best you can for the betterment of your child.

Most savvy parents will tell you:

Think of the rewarding moments in your life that your child has brought to you.

Keep the positive changes in your mind, let the negatives go, and you will be happy.

Chapter 23: Being A Single Parent Does Not Mean Raising An Unsteady Child

Teamwork is essential when it comes to the task of raising children.

Said teamwork is made much easier when the two parents are together and living under the same roof, as each can take turns with the responsibilities that go along with child-rearing while giving the other a chance to take a short break in the interim.

On the other hand, there is that group of single parents who do not have the luxury of relying on one another when it comes to the grind of daily life with the children.

As the divorce rate continues its upward climb, single parent families are seemingly becoming the norm. As a matter of fact, single parenting statistics cite that approximately 13.6 million adults in the United States are presently raising their minor children in the one-parent environment.

In many instances the occurrence of raising a child as a single parent is the outcome of a divorce in the family. As a result, the number of single father parenting households is on the rise.

Yet no matter how prevalent the situation of being a single parent has become, there are still several parenting myths that go along with the notion of bringing up a child by oneself.

First on the single parenting myth list is the idea that the mother will be rewarded with the custody of a child a majority of the time.

Though this notion might have been true ten or more years ago, much has changed in the field of family law since that time period. As long as both parents are mentally and physically healthy and stable, a judge will make a custodial decision based on the following factors:

- the amount of income each parent brings in;

- the safety of the residential area where each parent has made his or her home;

- the quality of the school districts in said areas;

- and other miscellaneous aspects that will aid the judge in making the right decision on behalf of the minor children.

Therefore, if it is the father who meets the above criteria more successfully than the mother, it should be expected that he is awarded primary custody of the couple's youngsters.

Next on the single parenting myth list is the belief that children in single parent homes have more behavioral problems than those adolescents who live with both their mother and their father.

It is true that the best scenario for any child enmeshed in the stages of growing up is to have his or her two parents present in the same household.

But if a child is being raised in a single parent atmosphere, this situation does not automatically turn that child into a disciplinary challenge. In other words, youngsters brought up by single parents are no more likely to abuse drugs or alcohol or receive bad grades in school than their peers living in homes where the parents are married, as many studies have shown.

The third myth regarding single parenting is the suggestion that a single parenting home is also a broken home.

Many spouses who have chosen to divorce have cited this decision as the reason why their homes are no longer considered "broken" - because after the divorce is final, the two warring parents are no longer situated under the same roof and consequently exposing their children to the perpetual fights between the adults.

It is not true that children in single parent families have lower self esteem than those adolescents living with both of their parents. Thus, this incorrect belief comprises the next single parenting myth.

One of the main factors that affects the self esteem of children is the income level of their parents.

For example, it is quite difficult for a child to watch as his friends receive all the hot toys on the market during the winter holidays, but because his parents (single or married) are in the bracket of lower earning he knows he won't see any of those toys for himself.

And since a two-parent family can be just as likely to experience income issues as a single parent family, the children from a single parent household are no more or less susceptible to self esteem problems than those from a family of two parents.

The fifth and final myth on the single parenting subject has to do with child support payments from one spouse to the other.

The amount of child support paid is based in part on the number of days of the year the paying parent spends with the minor children. If the two parents decide they want to share equal custody and therefore equal time with their children, the paid child support total will decrease as a result.

Does this mean the children suffer because the parent receiving the payments now has less money to spend when they are in her custodial care?

The answer to this question is also what debunks the myth.

Child support payments are doled out to compensate for the time the paying parent is not spending with the minor children.

To put it another way, if one parent has primary custody then he or she naturally spends more funds on the children, which is where the child support comes in to help cover that additional money spent.

But money cannot replace the time spent with a parent, which is why a child is better off having equal time with each adult in place of the payments his other parent would receive instead.

It is common knowledge that the ideal situation for children is to live with both parents.

Regardless, it is comforting to know that if a child must be brought up in a single parent home, he has just as much a chance of successfully thriving in his future life as a child who has both of his parents together on a daily basis.

Chapter 24: Single Dad With Toddler: Cutting Toxic Tv Time

Like most American parents, a single dad home alone with a toddler will probably seat his toddler comfortably on a baby chair and turn on the TV so the kid can watch his favorite cartoon channel while he does his house chores or attend to some personal calling. It is a fact that parents make use of the television to baby sit for them or use it as a pacifier.

What these parents don't know (or refuse to know) is that TV is toxic to infants and toddlers 2 years old and below. TV viewing for infants and toddlers robs them the chance to develop their own creative minds. It makes the kids too dependent on the boob tube for entertainment and prevents them from engaging in creative plays.

According to an advisory issued by the American Academy of Pediatrics, infants and toddlers watching too much TV negatively impacts their cognitive and language development and disturbs their regular sleeping patterns. Their study has also linked too much TV exposure during the first two years of the baby's life to greater health risks such as obesity, aggressive behavior, and ADHD.

ADHD, or Attention Deficit Hyperactivity Disorder, is a common psychiatric disorder affecting children. 9% of American children and 4.1% of American adults have been diagnosed with ADHD the symptoms of which include lack of focus, difficulty in paying attention, hyper activity, and difficulty in controlling behavior.

On the average, American children aged 1 to3 years old watch television 2 to 3 hours a day which by AAP standards is already child toxic and more than enough to put the child at risk of having the symptoms mentioned earlier. Unfortunately, the AAP stopped short at giving parents a warning and has not offered viable alternatives TV for entertaining or babysitting toddlers while their parents are busy with their chores.

This should not dampen your interest because there are really a lot of alternatives besides TV that can keep babies and toddlers entertained why you are busy doing something else. Do not forget that babies and toddlers are self-learners and they learn fast. They have the ability to create and engage in inner-directed plays - which in effect serves as the foundation of their learning.

We mistakenly think that there is always that need to stimulate a child or keep him entertained and so we do what we always do – put him in front of a TV – because that's what an adult will do to entertain themselves. The fact is we are unnecessarily occupying the baby's time and inhibit his natural urge to engage in his own activities and discover the world in his own terms.

The baby has the capacity to create and engage in her own independent play to entertain himself. Screen time prevents him from doing this. And worst, with screen time, we are not only branding his brains but we are also enslaving him to the boob tube while impairing his creative development.

Because infants can naturally initiate their own thoughts and activities, all we need to do is support and encourage them to cultivate these abilities- not with screen time, for God's sake – but by just letting him be. Simply give him play space and routinely leave him there – watching on the side of course. Babies learn best if we leave them to do their own thing. And as they grow older, all we need to do is to merely supply them with things they can use to self create their own independent plays. When they start to get bored with their own plays that would be the time to suggest what they can do.

Do not forget that not so long ago (before TV was invented) parents were able to keep their kids busy while they wash the dishes, clean the house, and attend to a hundred other household chores. It wasn't difficult then. It shouldn't be difficult now. Unless you want your kid to have branded brains, then it is best to heed the warnings of the child experts and keep them away from television – at least, during the first two years of their lives.

If you want some TV-free ideas on how to keep your toddlers pre-occupied and entertained as you go about your chores here they are:

Finger "Painting" (From Love Some)

This activity is perfect for 1 year old toddlers and up. The idea of finger painting may scare the wits out of you but this finger painting activity is mess-free and you won't need to keep a roll of paper towels ready. Get a zip lock bag and put several blobs of washable finger paint in it. Force the air out, lock, and seal with tape. Your toddler will enjoy pressing the blobs of paint and create different shapes for hours.

One Boy Band

This activity is good for 3 to 6 year old toddlers. Get your kid to bring out all his toy instruments. Line them up in a row and challenge your kid to create different compositions while going up and down the line of instruments and playing them. You can also challenge him to try and play two instruments simultaneously.

Make a Ball Maze (from A Happy Wanderer)

This activity is good for 2 year old and up toddlers. Make a maze using a large cardboard box and a lot of paper towel rolls. Cut the paper towel rolls in two and glue them (cascading down) the sides of the cardboard box. Let it dry and prop it up with a chair or anything to keep it tilted and in place. Give your kid some balls, or toy cars, or anything that rolls and let him drop them one at a time down the maze. This will keep him pre-occupied for hours.

If you are resourceful enough, you can find tons of these TV-free ideas on how to keep your toddlers entertained. Just keep on searching the net and select the ideas that are suitable to you and your child.

If you can't find the time to do this, then take out your iPhone and start downloading kid stuff applications like 'Wheels on the Bus', 'Smack Talk, and 'Scribble Lite' from the iPhone store. You will also find a lot of learn-to-read applications there. Teach your toddler how to play these games and it will keep him busy for hours. The only problem is you may not be able to get your iPhone back from him!

Chapter 25: On Being A Good Daddy The First Year

It's just a fact. Sometimes Dads are altogether comfortable with babies. While most Moms grew up playing with dolls and dreaming of having a real baby, such isn't usually the case when it comes to Dads. But with a few helpful pointers, you'll catch on to it and will be a pro in no time.

Getting to Know You

The best way to have a relationship with anyone is to spend quality time together getting to know them. Think about when you were first dating. You soaked in everything about this woman that is now the mother of your child. The same holds true when it comes to your little one. Spending time together will create a bond that will last a lifetime.

Here are some ways to spend time with your baby:

Take on a baby job, like bathing her or giving her evening bottle.

Interact when Mommy is busy.

Have some special things you do with your little one that are "Daddy things."

Let Mommy go somewhere and be the sole caretaker for a time.

Be confident! You have a spot no one else can fill!

Games Daddy's Play

Daddies are great at certain things... like play time. It may all seem like fun and games, but experts agree that play is serious business. Here are some ways in which your child will benefit from play, now and in the years to come:

Stimulates brain development.

Helps teach focus.

Develops motor skills.

Helps in weight control.

Develops hand-eye coordination.

Good for fine motor skills.

Helps develop visual tracking.

Is a great way to bond.

Play also helps your baby's cognitive and communication skills because it

Promotes reasoning.

Develops creative thinking.

Helps him plan and make decisions.

Is good for language skills.

Helps develop problem solving skills.

There are different kinds of play time with children of all ages. Some of the types of games for babies are:

Functional Play - Especially when your child begins to mimic, it's fun for him to imitate others through games.

Social Play - By social interaction, your little one can learn about social skills through laughter, smiles and looking. Peek-a-boo is a favorite.

Object Play - Touching, throwing, pushing and feeling objects help your little one learn sensory skills.

Role Play - While your little one won't master this type of play until he is around 30 months, it's still fun to play games that imitate different roles like doctor, Mommy, etc.

Symbolic Play - This form of play usually comes about around age two, but it's never too early to try it. Symbolic play is done by creating something out of nothing, pretending a shoe is a bus or that a box is a sled.

Games for Little Ones Before One

You may be at a loss as to what to play with a little baby. After all, football is out of the question… for now. Below you will find some age-appropriate games the two of you can play together that aren't too "baby-talk" oriented.

First Months

Bright Smiles Game

You may not even imagine it, but your infant is ready to play. She is learning to grasp objects and to focus on things. Take a bright toy and place it about 15 inches from her eyes. Move it around and "coo" at her. She will be delighted!

Peek-a-boo

Hide your face behind a blanket or even behind your hands. Appear and say, "Peek-a-boo!" The more animated, the better, as far as she's concerned.

Three to Six Months

Wheels on the Bus

Music is a big deal at this age as are hand motions. If you don't already know it, look up the song "Wheels on the Bus" and learn it so you and your little one can enjoy it together. Don't like that one? Any song you pick will be super if you add some hand motions.

Let's Dance!

Turn on your favorite music and dance with baby in your arms. This is one time the moves don't matter and long as you move!

Six to Nine Months

Smell This!

Your baby's sense of smell is coming alive. Play games that entice her sensory organs like smelling all sorts of things around the house like sweet scented candles, spices and even an apple.

Nine Months to One Year

Boxing

Now your baby is ready for some boxing. Well, maybe not the boxing you are thinking of but boxing, baby style. Take a good sized empty box and sit your baby in it, safely securing him inside. Pull or push the box around the room and listen to his joyous squeals.

Look Forward to a "One-derful" Year

You are not going to believe the fun you are going to have in the year to come. Your little "one" will playing more fun than you ever dreamed possible. You may even get to use the football!

Chapter Takeaways

Taking over a baby chore is a great way to be a good father.

Having a special time when you and your baby are alone helps you get to know one another.

Play is good for your little one's brain.

Playing you're your baby helps develop a strong bond between the two of you.

Dancing with your baby requires no skills and your baby will love it!

Conclusion

Thank you again for downloading this book!

I hope this book was able to help you deal with difficult and challenging toddlers. Whether your toddler is active or explosive, or both, these children somehow put immense strain on you as a parent. But that should not be the end of the world for you. The techniques that you have learned from this book will help you on your journey towards taming your child and eventually raise a kid that is well-mannered and well-behaved.

The next step is to try all these tips and techniques. Know what works for you and your toddler best. Remember, every day is a new learning experience. You may have challenging days and have somehow lost on those days, but know that you can rise up again and win over your flaws.

Parenting is a beautiful journey; something that you will take on for many years and yet will still miss especially when your children come of age and step out of the house. So be grateful that you still have time to nurture and be with them. You will surely miss those tantrums, diaper change, and all about this messy yet rewarding job called parenting.

Thank you and good luck!

www.ingramcontent.com/pod-product-compliance
Lightning Source LLC
Chambersburg PA
CBHW072008070526
44583CB00015B/1389